Complete Strangers

Mickeal Tanner

PublishAmerica
Baltimore

© 2009 by Mickeal Tanner
All rights reserved. No part of this book may be reproduced, stored in a retrieval system or transmitted in any form or by any means without the prior written permission of the publishers, except by a reviewer who may quote brief passages in a review to be printed in a newspaper, magazine or journal.

First printing

All characters in this book are fictitious, and any resemblance to real persons, living or dead, is coincidental.

PublishAmerica has allowed this work to remain exactly as the author intended, verbatim, without editorial input.

ISBN: 978-1-4489-9978-1
PUBLISHED BY PUBLISHAMERICA, LLLP
www.publishamerica.com
Baltimore

Printed in the United States of America

Complete Strangers

To the Reid Family,

From the family of one "unique snowflake" to another. ~~Enjoy~~ (kid grabbed pen while I tried to write "enjoy").

Enjoy

M. Thumz

To the Reich Chancery,

From the writer of one "major scientists"
to another. Being (not) asked for advice I
tried to write "us?").

(sig)

M. Planck

Prologue

This story came to me rather suddenly. It came without warning and it came without much fanfare. It is a true story, although I had never heard about it before I wrote about it. It was a complete surprise to me that the story turned out to be entirely true, word for word. I typically write about things I have seen before. Mostly I write about stories I have already heard or stories that have already been told. This story however had never been told and as such I was the explorer who came across it. Dilbert Douglas is a real person. Mind you, I have never actually met him, nor have I met anyone who has ever met him, nor have I met anyone who has ever heard of him, or any other character in this story, which is entirely true, because I heard it from a friend of mine.

Secondly, I would like to apologize now for what you will likely encounter through the course of this work. Firstly, I have never written a piece of this length and as such I am not used to entertaining anyone for this long a time period. I work best in short doses and unfortunately you are stuck with me for the next several hours, depending on how slow a reader you are. You could be stuck with me for the next several weeks if you are a slow reader, several months if you are a really slow reader, or, if you happen to be illiterate, the rest of your life. Now, this might not be a big deal if you have time to kill. I would say that my best customers would be people with a lot of time on their hands. Imprisoned criminals, long term hospital patients, the independently wealthy; these are the people who would have the time to make their way through this story and not attempt to kill me following its completion. If you have somewhere to be, DO NOT READ THIS BOOK.

Next up on the list of reasons not to read this book would be the absolute lack of credible research on any of the topics that I cover in this volume. For example, all research pertaining to medical issues are absolutely without credibility. Any research that I did conduct was based on the joys of Wikipedia. Wikipedia is a great research tool, and what makes it even better is that you can add anything that you want at anytime. For example, while doing some research, if you happen to come across something that doesn't make sense to you, you can just change it. Most of my research came from interviews conducted with the real people involved in story, far before I had actually met them.

Therefore, for those of you who are concerned with some of the details found within these pages, you need to talk to the sources. I am not the source. I am merely the purveyor of fine stories, although watered down. I will take complaints, although from a distance, but make no promises that it will create an apology, a change or anything else for that matter.

The Story

Dilbert Douglas woke up in a very confused state. Not the sort of confused state that would follow a nap or restless sleep or being suddenly and surprisingly awakened. Instead, Dilbert Douglas woke up in a very confused state because Dilbert Douglas had no idea who Dilbert Douglas was. He had no idea where he was; no idea how he got there and yet somehow knew that this was his home. It may have been the framed picture of himself in cap and gown at a graduation. It may have been the bottle of insulin in the bedside table in conjunction with the marks and sensitive parts of his body. As he rolled over in the bed he realized that he was not alone. Lying in bed beside him was a relatively attractive woman, likely in her mid thirties. Despite the fact that he had no idea who she was, nor did he in any way recognize her, Dilbert Douglas knew, (remembering of course that Dilbert Douglas did not know who Dilbert Douglas was) that her name was Susan and that she loved him.

Imagine for a moment that you had no idea who you were, no idea about your life. You did know that you had a wicked headache that seemed to get better whenever you ate certain sweet foods. Suddenly, Dilbert realized he was a diabetic. He rolled out of bed and decided that a shave and a shower were in order. He walked out of what he could only assume was his bedroom and begin to wander around the house looking for a bathroom. He somehow sensed that it was to his left and shockingly enough, it was. He walked into the tiled room and turned the shower on. He was almost sure that he liked to have a nice hot shower. So he left the shower on while he shaved.

While Dilbert trimmed the small goatee that speckled his chin, his mind wandered. It wandered to nothing in particular because obviously when you're an amnesiac, it's not like you're going to think back and find memories of your yesteryears. If you're an amnesiac you're thinking things like, 'I wonder if I'm allergic to shellfish' or 'how do I feel about religion'. At this juncture Dilbert became increasingly interested in whether he was Christian. More importantly, he became very interested in whether or not he was Jewish. Dilbert's sudden interest in Judaism did not stem from any solemn interest in the faith but rather he was somewhat concerned as to whether or not a lovely Jewish barber had taken 'a little off the top'. Upon confirming his belief in Jesus Christ and the subsequent thanks and praise heaped upon said Christ, Dilbert brought his attention back to the job he was doing shaving his face.

If you have never before shaved your face, let me explain something to you. When you drag a sharp razor blade across the speed bumps you call a beard, slicing off a few pieces of face meat is always a concern. And as Dilbert refocused his attention he realized that he was a victim of said, self-induced torture. There were several small nicks and cuts on his face and neck. He applied small pieces of tissue to the affected areas but it did not seem to do anything. He applied more and more tissue while more and more blood poured out of the holes he had personally perforated. The tissue was soon replaced with towels and Dilbert continued to bleed. The other problem with all this of course would be that if you have low blood sugar and then low blood, this means an even lower blood sugar level. This means that Dilbert Douglas went from standing, to sitting, to kneeling, to lying, to dreaming.

Dilbert Douglas dreamt his life. He dreamt who he was, who his girlfriend was, his job, his house, his life. He dreamt of the day he graduated university with a degree in physics. He dreamt of his first date with Ellen and came to realize that his previous assertion that the pretty nude woman in his bed was in fact named Susan, was in fact, wrong. She was, in fact, named Ellen. Dilbert learned more and more about himself as the dream wore on and, upon waking forgot his girlfriend's name was Ellen, forgot where, when and that they met. He forgot where he went to school, that he went to school, that he took physics in school and that physics existed along with the intricate laws of gravity, inertia and other brilliant ideas. All that being said, had Dilbert known anything (or remembered in this case) about physics, he would have understood that he was lying on the tiled floor of his (he assumed it was his) bathroom floor because when he passed out, gravity took over. He also would have realized that the reason it took so much energy for him to lift himself off the floor was that objects in motion, stay in motion, objects at rest, stay at rest and Dilbert Douglas was most definitely at rest.

Dilbert Douglas made his way to his feet slowly. He had a headache, his face was covered in blood, he had a desperate craving for something sweet and he had no idea where he was. He looked into the mirror and thought, "Dilbert, you'd better figure out what is going on here." Actually, since Dilbert Douglas had no idea who Dilbert Douglas was, he actually thought, "guy in mirror, I'm confused." It was at this point that Dilbert, referred to as guy in mirror, decided that a shower was in order. The water was already running for him when he got in. Dilbert figured that he must have forgotten (ironic isn't it) to pay the water bill because he could not get any hot water. He of course did not realize that the hot water was out because while he lay bleeding on the floor, dreaming of a life he could not remember, he used all the hot water. So Dilbert Douglas had a very brief, very cold shower.

Emerging from the showers icy grasp, Dilbert toweled off and, determining that he would probably not figure out the details of his life anytime soon, he decided to deal with his primal instincts, one at a time. The next primal instinct that Dilbert had was to find food, preferably sweet. He sensed that the kitchen was down the hall and to his right and was amazed to discover that he was right. He opened up his fridge in search of something sweet and discovered a jug of orange juice that would fulfill his need for sweet and uncovered some ham, a jar of mayonnaise and some slices of bread that would constitute a sandwich, fulfilling his need for sustenance. Washing the sandwich down with a nice big glass of orange juice, Dilbert then tried to determine what exactly he was going to do next.

Imagine the conundrum that Dilbert now faced. He had no idea what he was interested in, no idea what he liked and no idea what he did for a job, if he even had a job. It would take an intense amount of personal reflection to solve these problems. Luckily, Ellen took this intense moment of personal reflection as her queue to enter the room.

"Morning sweetie," exclaimed Ellen as she headed into the room her somewhat confused boyfriend was currently located in. She wore what Dilbert could only assume was one of his shirts. It covered her torso and her hips, leaving Dilbert with a glimpse of her white cotton underwear. For the second time that day, blood rushed to some part of Dilbert's anatomy and once again he felt very woozy.

"Good morning," replied Dilbert with a very thoughtful, measured pause. He paused for several reasons. The first was that he was unsure of the exact time of day, as he had simply started awake on the bathroom floor. More importantly he paused because he had no idea who this woman wearing a man's (presumably his) dress shirt and white cotton panties was nor why she was walking into this (presumably his) living room.

"Did you sleep well," she asked?

"I think so. I don't really remember. I sort of woke up on the bathroom floor."

"What? You know Dilbert, if you don't get your narcolepsy looked into, you could really hurt yourself."

Now the first thought that went through Dilbert's head was, 'she knows me. This very attractive woman who is wearing what I am assuming is my dress shirt and a pair of deliciously beautiful white cotton panties knows me. Furthermore, I am apparently her sweetie.' This thought was very important to Dilbert, which is why it is so interesting that it quickly disappeared, replaced by an even more important and interesting thought. 'Oh my god. I'm a narcoleptic. What am I going to do? How will I live my life shouldering the incredible burden of narcolepsy?' This second thought, important and interesting as it may have been, was pushed out of Dilbert's head as quickly as the first when Dilbert came upon the third epiphany. This third thought, epiphany if you will, was, 'what the hell is narcolepsy? How am I going to live my life shouldering the incredible burden of having narcolepsy and having no idea what the hell this crippling disability is, nor knowing how to deal with it?' The third thought was dwarfed by the complexities, ramifications and incredible repercussions of the fourth thought. This thought would have paralleled the discoveries of Newton, Einstein or even Ron Jeremy (if Dilbert could remember who these people were or what discoveries they had made). The fourth thought, thundering through Dilbert's brain life a frigate was as follows; 'My name is Dilbert.' With this epiphany, Dilbert fell unexpectedly asleep.

Dilbert Douglas woke up slouched over on the couch, the most minute of driblets spilling out of the left side of his mouth. He felt sated so he could only assume that he had recently eaten. The more important issue was that he had no idea who he was or where he was. He looked around and found that he was in a fairly well furnished home with nice lighting and a big screen TV. Using that most carnal of male thought processes, he decided to watch some television. He picked up the remote and began flicking through channels and channels that he did not think he really had any interest in. He did briefly find interest in a news broadcast discussing local news stories until he realized he didn't even know for sure what country he lived in, let alone the local area where this news would be occurring. He finally settled on a music television channel where he watched a few recent, (well, recent for him) music videos. It was during one of these music videos that Dilbert learned something very important. When someone with epilepsy watches vibrant, flashing strobe lights, often found in music videos, something happens. Dilbert's eyes rolled back in his head and he began to experience his first (as far as he knew) seizure. As he began to thrash around his (even I'm going to assume its his living room for the sake of the flow of the story) living room, another amazing thing happened. Dilbert Douglas remembered who he was. After the seizure subsided,

Dilbert Douglas began to dance around his living room (now knowing it was in fact his living room) singing out invented lyrics at the top of his lungs. His 'song' went something like this, 'June 19th, 1973 is the year that I was born. In a small town outside Calgary, where I went to high school and university. My favorite food is sweet and sour chicken balls and my favorite drink is scotch and water, easy on the water. I don't like tomatoes but I love pasta sauce, Oh I love being Dilbert Douglas.' At this point, Dilbert expelled all his energy and proceeded to pass out from a combination of diabetic exhaustion, epileptic fatigue and narcoleptic… narcolepsy.

When Dilbert awoke he had no idea where he was, or who he was but he felt sad and tired and a little sore, as he had bitten his tongue, although he had no idea how or why. The television was on so he decided to go ahead and watch some boob tube. However, since he didn't know what he wanted to watch, he turned it off and wandered into the kitchen where he opened the fridge and decided that as a snack, he would drink a glass of O.J and take some ham, mayo and bread and create a sandwich. He devoured the sandwich and washed it down with a nice, big glass of orange juice. After his meal, Dilbert decided to get some fresh air. He was not sure when the last time he had been outside was but he sensed it had not been recently. He did however face a conundrum. The best place for Dilbert to be, since he knew nothing about himself, was home. And while he did want to leave home and get some fresh air, he had no idea where he lived or how to get anywhere. He found a pair of keys and discovered they worked for his front door. He then checked the numbers beside his front door and discovered that he lived at 918. Although he was still a little unsure as to what street he lived on, he looked down to his left and about a half a block down he found a sign that said Maine Street, (note the spelling). So, Dilbert Douglas, (despite the fact that he didn't know he was Dilbert Douglas) lived at 918 Maine Street, (note the spelling). He decided that he would only make left turns on his way out, followed by only right turns to get him back. And with that, Dilbert Douglas set out to discover his surroundings.

COMPLETE STRANGERS

It was in fact a beautiful fall day when Dilbert Douglas set out to discover the subtle nuances of the city he called home (or at least he assumed he called this city, or possibly town, village, burg or hamlet home. To be honest, it seemed a moot point given the severity of his other concerns).

So out he set, down Maine Street until he came to Sutton Ave, and having already passed several streets, he decided to take this one. Sutton Avenue turned out to be a lovely street. There were several interesting looking shops but given the fact that he was wearing a pair of jeans he found on his floor and a t-shirt that smelled okay, so okay that he thought it might belong to a woman, and given the fact that he had not found any money in his (he presumed his) house before he left, he had neither the look to enter most of these high end looking shops nor the money with which to procure anything he found of interest, Dilbert continued down Sutton avenue without further distraction.

Arriving at the next street corner, Sutton Avenue and James Street, further distraction was unleashed. At this particular street corner Dilbert Douglas met a lovely young woman by the name of Ellen. Dilbert knew this woman's name was Ellen because she was wearing a nametag that said, "Ellen." It was of course possible that she was a member of the witness protection program, or that she had a name tag fetish, but the more likely conclusion to come to was that this woman, who was walking towards Dilbert Douglas with a smile that resembled recognition, was in fact named Ellen.

"Hey babe, where ya headed," asked the lovely young woman named Ellen, further proving that she knew Dilbert by calling him babe and also by the quick peck on the cheek she gave him.

"Actually... Ellen, I was just going for a little walk around the neighborhood. Where are you headed?" This seemed to be an appropriate answer for the situation.

"Just going to Steve's' for a couple of hours between shifts. Oh hey, can you pick up something for dinner tonight? I'm not going to get a chance."

"I would have no problem with that, IF I had brought my wallet." Dilbert accompanied this with a frown, supremely indicative of his dismay.

"No problem. I have cash on me." Ellen rooted through her purse and pulled out several crumpled up $20 bills. She handed them to Dilbert. "I have to get to Steve's', but I will see you tonight, ok."

Dilbert decided that since he was quite sure that he was dating this woman and he would probably not remember her in the very, very near future, it was time to spice up his love life. Dilbert leaned in for the kiss to end all kisses. She responded by leaning in for an equally passionate smooch. And with that, Dilbert was once again very alone in the city, or town, or village, or whatever this place was.

Once more, as has become the clear pattern in Dilbert's life, he had a problem. He was well aware that by following a series of carefully planned right turns, he could return home, but the woman with the wonderful red lips, (and although he didn't know it equally wonderful white cotton panties) had asked him to do something. She had asked him to do something that, for most people, should have been easy. But in Dilbert's case, (who once more was unaware that his name was Dilbert) it was a struggle, to say the least. Firstly, he was unaware what he might like. He did not know if he liked Italian or Thai, if he was allergic to shellfish or peanuts, or even if he preferred chicken or fish. Furthermore, the second of his conundrums on the food front was that he had no idea what Ellen liked. He had no idea what she didn't like. And he had no idea what could possibly be lethal to her. I mean, imagine there is a wonderful woman with beautiful brown eyes, an absolutely button-nose cute haircut reminiscent of the late 1970's and two beautiful round breasts that were achingly luscious. Now imagine that this delicious female has asked you to proceed with a very simple request. But, by fulfilling this incredibly simple and easy request, you could in fact kill her. Imagine that this is a woman who loves you, or at least likes you an awful lot, and through the simple process of making her supper, you would end any and all chance of possibly sleeping with her. Here lies the conundrum.

These issues did not compare with the other major component of the problem. Mainly, that Dilbert Douglas had no idea where he could in fact use the money that Ellen had provided him in order to procure food. While Dilbert had not been looking specifically for food on his way to meet Ellen, (sort of on his way to meet Ellen), he had not happened upon any in his wanderings. So, the quest for food began anew, using only left turns. Left turns and left turns only would be the manner in which Dilbert Douglas would find food. He could only hope that the engineers of the city, or village, or hamlet, (oh for the love of God the story takes place in Boston), designed the city so that he could easily get to a grocery store using only left turns.

So Dilbert walked and contemplated supper. He contemplated the concept of making supper and realized the following facts. He had no idea what utensils or cookware he had. While most people had a lot of these, Dilbert wondered if he might be one of those rich, eccentric people who only ever ate out and did not own any cooking supplies. He was also concerned about ingredients. I mean, its one thing to pick up some chicken and some rice and make a lovely Indian chicken dish. But what if you don't have curry, or any spices? You will be making an extremely dull meal. Also, when you think about it, not a lot of people die from eating at a fast food restaurant. At least not from eating there once or twice. So Dilbert thought, it might be best to pick up something at one of the fast food restaurants he saw off in the distance.

As the grease began to waft into Dilbert's nostrils, his mind began to change. He began to question why Ellen would give him eighty dollars for him to purchase burgers and fries and a couple of milkshakes. And the quest for food continued. Burger King and McDonald's gave way to Boston Pizza and Ruby Tuesday and these gave way to upscale restaurants that had names that resonated off your tongue like fizz off a rum and coke. Places like, Desch and Bella Vita. And so Dilbert finally walked into a restaurant called Michael's. It was nice. Nice is actually an understatement. It was very nice. Actually, that too is an understatement. Michael's was an absolutely fantastic restaurant. It was beautiful. It was marvelous. It was ethereal. And Dilbert Douglas walked in like a man who knew what he wanted and said to the hostess, "I have no idea what I want and I desperately need your help."

The hostess was polite. She was sweet and kind and very polite.

"Well sir, what kind of food do you like? We have steaks, seafood and pasta. What is your favorite?"

"Well, you see, that's sort of the problem. I have no idea. To be honest, I don't even know who I am."

Kerri, (the hostesses name was Kerri), still feigned politeness but this politeness was mixed with concern now. Was this man crazy? Was this man insane? Was he deranged or in some other way damaged?

"What do you mean sir?"

"Well, I woke up this morning and I had no idea who I was. Or where I was. Or anything else really. So, I decided to go for a walk, and I bumped into my girlfriend Ellen. She told me that she wanted me to go get supper because she would not have time. So, she gave me eighty dollars and told me to pick up supper. So, that's what I'm trying to do."

It was obvious that Kerri's politeness was being replaced with confusion, dismay and a small measure of fear. And yet, she composed herself, pulled herself together if you will, and asked the only logical question.

"How do you know this woman Ellen is your girlfriend if you don't know who you are?"

It was a good question. It was clear and concise and broached what was, at this time, one of the main concerns. Really, when it came down to it, the idea of a man who did not know who he was, or who his girlfriend was and his girlfriend, who knew who both of them were, was astoundingly complex. It was beyond complex. It was ridiculous. It was beyond ridiculous. Everything about the entire situation was complex and ridiculous. It was a complex and ridiculous situation and neither Dilbert, who had no idea who he or Kerri was, nor Kerri, who at least knew who one of them was, was able to come to terms with the complexities, or the ridiculousness. So, they went with what they could handle.

"Alright sir. Well, I would recommend pasta. Pasta is hard to go wrong with. I like pasta. I'm sure you'll like pasta and I would venture to say that Ellen would probably like pasta. I don't suppose that along with your amazing knowledge of her name you happen to know if she might be vegetarian?"

"That is a really good point. I have no idea."

"Well, then you should get at least one vegetarian dish and one with meat probably. We have a lovely linguini in a cream sauce with fresh sautéed vegetables. We also have a delicious chicken bowtie pasta with chives that I think you would really like, if you eat meat, which no one, including you, even knows. Which means, you can eat meat and you would have no idea if it was the first time you had ever eaten it." With this Kerri paused to once again ponder the absurdity of the situation. "Are you even curious as to who you are? I mean, if it were me, I would want to know what the fuck was going on. How can you just sit here ordering food when you don't have a sweet clue who the fuck you are. I mean, you could be a billionaire. Or homeless."

"Oh no, I have a house. I woke up there this morning and all the clothes seemed to fit so I am pretty sure it was my house. And it was nice, but it wasn't billionaire nice unless it was like, a small place I had for taxation reasons or something. But all in all, I don't think I am a billionaire. I guess I could be, but I don't think so. Why am I doing this? Ellen asked me to. I guess that's all it took."

"I wish that's all it took with my boyfriend. My boyfriend would have to get kicked in the junk just to get off the couch. Anyways, as your guide on this foray into unknown food horizons, I shall pick your food. I shall ensure that it comes to less than eighty dollars and it will be ready in about ten minutes. So, you have a seat, and I will be back."

Dilbert took Kerri's advice and had a seat. While sitting there, he contemplated what Kerri had said. He was possibly the greatest boyfriend in the history of the world. I mean, everyone else would have been worried about where they were going and why. Everyone else would be concerned about who they were and what their life was like. But Dilbert Douglas, (who was absofuckinglutely unaware that he was

Dilbert Douglas), took the eighty dollars his girlfriend, (presumably his girlfriend), had given him, went to the nearest really nice restaurant he could find and ordered a delicious dinner for two which would likely get him laid, possibly for the first time, possibly for the last time. Who knew? But what Dilbert Douglas did know was that he needed to get this food and get home, before he forgot how awesome he was.

While Dilbert contemplated his stupendousness in the foyer of Michael's, Kerri tried desperately to explain the story of Dilbert to the chef who was now preparing Dilbert's supper. As chefs are wont to do, Chef Andre was so self absorbed in the flambéed chicken and the sautéed mushrooms and peppers that he never really got into the story, thus missing out on a unique piece of business. Luckily, Kerri's boyfriend Charles was also a chef so Kerri was aware of the absolute neglect chefs had for anything not directly related to the task at hand. While it was an interesting fact that the soon to be devourer of Andre's flambéed chicken had no idea what flambéed chicken was, nor any other sort of chicken for that matter, it had no bearing on how much tumeric or cumin he would add to his dishes.

Going through Andre's mind were recipes, variations, ingredients, menus, dishes, restaurants, chefs, waitresses, hostesses and desserts. Meanwhile, going through Dilbert's mind was nothing. Not the nothing that comes from drifting in and out of this thought or that but the nothing that comes from having no idea what thoughts you could possibly drift in and out of. One thought began making its way through Dilbert's mind. Luckily, due to the lack of traffic, it made its way quickly through Dilbert's head and into his stomach. It started as a grumble and then it turned into a direct need, a need for something sweet. Dilbert was not sure why he had this craving for sweetness, because Dilbert Douglas was unaware that he was a diabetic. He was, however, acutely aware that he needed something sweet. He got up from his seat in the foyer of Michael's and made his way to the hostess stand. Kerri was still in the kitchen, discussing Dilbert with Andre, but there was a small bowl of mints. They were the kind of mints that come wrapped in small white plastic with the name of the restaurant written on them in fancy red script. So Dilbert popped one of them, not the wrapper but the mint, into his mouth. Rather than suck, he bit and chewed, crushing the mint with his teeth, breaking them into a thousand fine powdery pieces. He devoured the mint as though he had never eaten in his entire life, although he did recall a lovely meal of a ham sandwich and some OJ before leaving his home. After having crushed the first mint, Dilbert worked on the second, and the third, and the fourth. The feeling of craving sweetness was replaced by a different feeling. It was not as you might think, the feeling of satiation. It was not a feeling of filling oneself up or meeting the desire. It was instead a feeling of recognition. Dilbert REMEMBERED mints. He remembered what they tasted like, what they felt like and what they smelled like. He did not remember this from what he tasted now but out of his actual memory came storming this wild recollection of a particular good mint, following a particularly scrumptious meal. He recalled eating the most beautiful steak, drenched in the most beautiful marinade, dripping with flavor. He remembered the flavor so clearly that he wanted to get up and tell Kerri that what he wanted more than anything else, more than flambéed chicken or sautéed vegetables, was a steak. He wanted a steak so bad that his mind ached. His limbs began to quiver in anticipation of the steak that would soon meet his lips in an embrace of meat and carnivore. Then, Dilbert remembered something else. Dilbert remembered why he should not eat mints, or any overly sweet foods without the use of insulin. Dilbert Douglas remembered that he was diabetic at about the same time that Kerri wandered back to her post. As the beautiful young woman emerged from the kitchen, she was greeted with an alarming scene. The man who had only recently informed her that he had no idea who he was, also apparently had no idea how not to pass out. Because he was currently lying on the floor of Michael's frothing at the mouth.

    The ambulance ride was fun, as ambulance rides go. Dilbert was barely conscious of his surroundings but a new sensation surrounded him; familiarity. Dilbert Douglas knew who he was, and this excited him to a degree one cannot imagine. It excited him so much so that the paramedics believed that he was going into cardiac arrest and increased the oxygen flow. This caused more oxygen to make its way to Dilbert's brain, filled now with memories of birthdays, and Labor Days and love affairs and premature ejaculations. This may seem like an odd combination of events, but if you knew Dilbert's history, it would make perfect sense. However, as oxygen filled his brain, it pushed all these ideas out. He lost Jennifer West, Connor Andrews, softball, the mumps and the 1997 World Series. He still had autumn, but now that was gone too. He had a glimmer of The Catcher in The Rye but it was now lost to gasping for air. Finally, Dilbert Douglas and his entire history exhaled. And Dilbert Douglas, no longer knowing who Dilbert Douglas was, slept.

When Dilbert Douglas awoke, he heard chatter. He heard voices, whispers and small talk. "2cc pentha… 5 o clock… I know, I can't believe she's with him eith… No wallet, no id… new washer and dryer from her parents." He heard this small talk and he also heard a rather constant and consistent beeping noise. He quickly ascertained that he was either in a coffee shop or a hospital. The beeping could be the coffee maker, the chit chat that of the baristas and their regular crew. This did not in any way explain why he was lying down or why he had several tubes and plugs connecting to various intersections of his body. It was definitely a hospital probably. This was further confirmed by the doctor who walked into the room. Sure, he could have also been a barista, but he did have the white coat. Perhaps his words would serve as some sort of final indication as to where Dilbert, (man in bed who did not know who he was), currently resided.

"Sir, you're in a hospital." There. That wasn't so hard, was it?

"What happened?"

"You were waiting in a restaurant and you went into diabetic shock. Do you remember that at all?"

"I don't remember anything."

"That's typical sir of diabetic shock."

"No, I don't remember anything. I don't know who I am. I don't know anything about me. I don't remember going into shock or any other aspect of my life. I don't remember anything."

"I'm not sure I understand. You're saying that you have no idea who you are. You don't know anything about your life, at all?"

"That is exactly what I am saying."

"That's fucked up."

"You're telling me"

"Sorry sir, that was very unprofessional of me. It's just that those tend to be more stories of books than of real life. I have never encountered an actual amnesiac. Well, we need to figure out who you are."

Dilbert sort of assumed he had been spending most of his day doing exactly that. He was a minute portion amazed at the idiocy that this doctor represented. Had he remembered more of his life, he would have remembered that this doctor seemed actually quite a bit smarter than most doctors he had encountered. There was the doctor who had given him penicillin, after he had read the file that said Dilbert was allergic to penicillin. There was the doctor who had told him that it was nothing to worry about. This was the same doctor he saw two days later for a check up, after his appendix burst. In fact, Dilbert's life was littered with doctors who had been unable or unwilling to assist him. So, he should not have been surprised that this doctor was somewhat of an idiot. But then again, Dilbert didn't know anything about his medical history and as such could not have known that this doctor was slightly smarter than the average bear.

"Is there a particular way we could go about doing that? I mean, is there some sort of database that has my fingerprints in it or something?"

"Well, we could check the records, but typically the databases are police databases so unless you've committed a crime they would not be able to help us. And if you've committed a crime, maybe you don't want to be found."

Dilbert had not even considered this. Maybe he was the kingpin of an international crime organization. Maybe there was a hit out on him and in order to keep him out of trouble he had erased his own memory. That was ridiculous. No one would erase their own memory. Or would they? No, they would not. So he was not an international crime kingpin who had erased his memory on purpose in order to avoid assassination. But what if he was an international crime kingpin whose memory had been erased by accident as a result of an assassination attempt? That was entirely plausible. Or what if one of the rival families had erased his memory to keep him away from his fortune. I mean, someone could easily have decided that Dilbert Douglas, (mind you an odd name for a crime kingpin, but then again, he didn't know his name was Dilbert Douglas. It could have been Stephano Magellen) had been the head of the Magellen crime family long enough and now it was time for some new up and comer, perhaps a nephew, to take over the family business. Yes, this was most definitely the case. But if this was the case, then perhaps the doctor was right and he would not want to look in these databases to see who he was. On the other hand, perhaps instead of mob syndicate kingpin, he was in fact a pizza deliveryman who had merely bumped his head too hard. And if it turned out that he was Stephano Magellen, head of the Magellen crime family, he could probably buy his way out of prison anyways.

"Well, I don't think that I am some sort of crime family kingpin. I would very much like to find out who I am, so let's do these tests."

The doctor, Dilbert found out that his name was Dr. Wilkes, put him through a battery of tests, not only to determine who he was, but also to figure out what was wrong with him. They ran tests upon tests. In some cases, they ran tests on some of the tests they were running. They tried to determine what else might be wrong with Dilbert. Sure, he was a diabetic, but they also had to try to figure out what was causing this amnesia. They found that when they pricked his finger for one of the tests, he bled and bled and bled. They checked for clotting agents and found that there were few. They discovered something that Dilbert had discovered earlier that day, only he didn't remember having done so. They discovered that Dilbert Douglas, along with being a diabetic, was a hemophiliac. Dilbert was confused. He thought he liked women. He had yet to see one, but he had a vague notion of liking women. He was not attracted to the doctor, and the doctor was an attractive man. He was handsome. He was tall, with short, carefully coifed brown hair. He was well built. He was not overly muscular, but he had very little fat on his body. He was a handsome man, but Dilbert was not sexually attracted to him. So, when they told him that he was a hemophiliac, he was confused. Then they explained that a hemophiliac was someone who had little or no clotting agents in their blood, not someone who liked members of the same sex for sexual interaction.

Thus Dilbert began to understand a little about himself. He now understood that he was a diabetic, which meant that his body could not control his blood sugar level and he now understood that he was a hemophiliac which did not mean that he liked long walks on the beach and Elton John but instead meant that he would bleed and bleed and bleed if left unchecked. But he still did not know that his name was Dilbert Douglas and that his girlfriend Ellen was currently very much confused that Dilbert Douglas was not sitting at home with her supper. Of course, Dilbert was unaware that Ellen was waiting for supper and furthermore that Ellen even existed. So, Dilbert did not feel late, although he most definitely was.

Ellen was also late, but not in quite the same way. Ellen was late for a very important monthly date with her menstrual cycle. This fact, combined with her hunger and annoyance that Dilbert had taken her eighty dollars and not procured supper, meant that Ellen was now late, pregnant and angry. She was not angry in the "I can't believe Gray's Anatomy is not on this week" way or even in the "I didn't want chicken, I wanted fish" way but rather in the, "I am going to rip your heart out using my bare hands and then throw your heart up against a brick wall before finally crushing your entire soul with the spiky heel of those four inch stilettos you really like but instead of being excited that they make my legs look amazingly hot you'll be dead because I will have destroyed your heart" way. So, Ellen took her remaining crumpled up twenty dollar bills and made her way to McDonald's for a double cheeseburger with extra pickles, pickles being the first of her newly discovered hormone induced cravings. This all took place while Dilbert had a prostate exam which, had Ellen been aware of it, would have made her very happy. She was all prepared to tell him to take supper and shove it up his ass, and falling from the sky had been an extraordinarily similar gift.

Dilbert was uncomfortable. He was extremely uncomfortable. Partly because he was absolutely confused about who he was, what his favorite color was and what the hell was going on in his life. However, he was also partly uncomfortable because Dr. Wilkes had extremely wide fingers. This would have been fine if they were shaking hands, or if they were thumb wrestling. This would have been fine if they were playing playstation or if they were shuffling cards. But they were doing none of these things. Dilbert was bent over a table and Dr. Wilkes had his fingers inside of Dilbert's ass, playing tinkle me pick with his prostate. Dilbert was extremely uncomfortable. He tried to express his discomfort to the doctor but what came out was a slightly muffled moan. It was all he could muster.

Ellen was halfway to McDonalds when she came to a startling realization. What if Dilbert was hurt? He was an epileptic, a narcoleptic, and a hemophiliac. A number of scenarios shot through Ellen's mind. What if he decided to go to a strobe light store and was now thrashing around on the floor of Tom' Strobe and Stuff? What if he had been looking for a new mattress and while testing them out, had fallen asleep, and then discovered that the mattress store was actually a front for rave party, and after he fell asleep they brought out the strobe lights, sending him into a vicious seizure? Or, and this was possibly the worst possible scenario, what if he was shopping for new kitchen utensils and while shopping, the store manager turned on a strobe light at the precise moment when Dilbert was walking past the knife section. What if the strobe lights sent him into a seizure, the result of which was his absolute exhaustion, the result of which was he falling into a narcoleptic, epileptic seizure? And what if he fell DIRECTLY ON THE KNIVES? Oh god, thought Ellen. I have to get to a hospital, NOW.

While Ellen was better acquainted with who she was, there were still certain questions in regards to her character. You see, while Ellen was well aware that she was Ellen Duncan, she was also well aware that she was Monica Anderson. You see, while Ellen was not an amnesiac she did have two distinct and separate personalities. One of these personalities was a lovely young waitress by the name of Ellen Duncan.

COMPLETE STRANGERS

Ellen was from Manchester, England but had moved to the US when she was still a baby. Her parents had raised her in a small farming community outside Topeka, Kansas. She was a very happy child. She was a very well liked, well-adjusted child with many friends. But when Ellen was very young, she had a best friend. Her best friend was a young girl named Monica Anderson. Monica lived several blocks away but always seemed able to make time for Ellen. Ellen's parents did not have much time for her. But Monica always did. The only problem was that Monica was not a real person. Like many young children, even myself, Ellen had an imaginary friend. This was fine when Ellen was 5. This was fine when Ellen was 7. And this was even fine when Ellen was 9. However, it was not fine when Ellen turned 17. It was not fine when Ellen actually began talking to Monica when people were around. People began to think somewhat differently about Ellen. Rather than "well-liked" and "well-adjusted," people began to think of her as "crazy" and "kind of loopy." This was quite a change for Ellen and rather than causing her to "break up" with her friend Monica, it had quite the opposite reaction. Rather than the pair becoming two, the two became one. Ellen Duncan, quite often, talked with a South Boston accent, just like her good friend Monica Anderson. Ellen Duncan, quite often liked tomatoes, just like her good friend Monica Anderson. And from time to time, Ellen Duncan introduced herself as Monica Anderson, just like her good friend Monica Anderson. It was enough to make the average person believe that Ellen Duncan had gone insane. Unfortunately for her, Ellen's parents were actually somewhat more uptight than the average person. So, they sent her to live in a lovely little institution just outside Boston.

Sunrise Junction, (I know, I know. It's a ridiculous name for anything, let alone a mental institution, but I swear it's the real name), was a very funny place where everyone wore a funny, funny face, where the streets are paved with gold, and no one ever grows old. For those of you who are thinking, that line sounds familiar; it is from a Wizard of Oz cartoon that was on early mornings in the late 1980's. And that is the kind of loonyness that Ellen was subjected to at Sunrise Junction. (I mean this in both the literal and figurative sense.) Not only were the patients forced to swallow tripe about how wonderful a place

Sunrise Junction was, they were also forced to watch shows like The Wizard of Oz, Punky Brewster, and occasionally, if they were extraordinarily well-behaved, Alf. Sunrise Junction was an interesting place. The doctors were actually pretty good, unlike the lovely Dr. Wilkes, and Ellen actually liked it there. However, Ellen Duncan was not cured. She learned to hide when she was Monica, pretending to be someone she was not. But she was never cured and, in her most trying times, Ellen was always rescued by Monica. Monica was a lovely girl and not quite as sensitive as Ellen was. Where Ellen would break, Monica would barely bend. Where Ellen would cry, Monica would laugh, and then scream "fuck you" at the top of her lungs. So, now, when Ellen needed Monica the most, Monica led the way to the hospital. It is at this time interesting to note that while Dilbert had never met Ellen, as far as he knew, although then again, he had also never met Dilbert, Monica had never met Dilbert. Two people, who don't know each other, looking for each other. Its bound to work out, right?

Dilbert had been poked and prodded over and over again. They had determined many things about Dilbert Douglas but they were still unable to determine that he was Dilbert Douglas. They had determined that he was not a major player in a crime syndicate or, if he was, he was very good at hiding his identity. It was doubtful. They had checked him in every major database. What amazed Dr. Wilkes more than anything was Dilbert's nonchalant mannerisms. If it were me or you and we were in the hospital with no idea who we were, we'd be screaming blue murder. I would punch people in the face, one at a time, until someone told me who I was. Someone had to know. Someone had to recognize me. Someone had to have gone to high school or university with me. But Dilbert Douglas was quite a different person. Dilbert was calm and relaxed, almost too relaxed. Dilbert was relaxed to the point where it worried Dr. Wilkes.

"August, why is it that you are so calm about this whole situation? You must know that most people would be extremely concerned, almost deranged with anger and confusion if they didn't know who they were. But you are not. You are cool, calm and collected, and that makes me concerned, almost deranged with anger and confusion." Dr. Wilkes could simply not imagine what was going on in Dilbert's head.

Right now you are probably wondering who the hell August is. August is Dilbert Douglas. Dilbert Douglas is August. Dr. Wilkes was tired of calling Dilbert sir, or guy who doesn't know who he was, so he decided that Dilbert needed a name, even if only a temporary one, and since it was August 14th, 2008, August seemed like a perfectly acceptable name. Dilbert had no problem with this. As has been clearly demonstrated, Dilbert didn't really have any problems with anything. He was a very kind and sweet man who just wanted everyone to be happy. He was less concerned with his own happiness than he was with the happiness of others. Generally, we see this as a fantastically wonderful character trait, but in Dilbert's case, (or August's case. Hell, you could call him Sue if you wanted to and he wouldn't give two shits), it was emblematic of his whole problem. If Dilbert wasn't going to try to figure out who he was, who was? Sure, Dr. Wilkes would continue to plug away but without the help of Sue, this would become increasingly difficult.

Monica Anderson approached the hospital with the grace and fragility of an 18th century freight train. She was loud and obnoxious and you had the idea that she could derail at any moment. She approached the reception area and rather than waiting in line, she simply walked past several people, one of who was bleeding from the ear, and said "I'm looking for my friend's boyfriend. His name is Dilbert Douglas. Is he here?"

There were, of course, a number of problems with the whole scenario. Firstly, Dilbert Douglas was in that very hospital but no one had any idea. Secondly, if by some random chance August and Monica did bump into one another, neither one would have a sweet clue. Thirdly, August was on the 8th floor and unless Monica happened to stumble through every floor in a random quest for a random person, the odds were stacked against them. Fourthly, and finally, Peg Burrows, the receptionist at this fine institution, hated when people did not stay in line, stay in order. As such, when Monica pushed past bleeders and criers and waiters and decided to verbally vomit her request to Peg, she deeply offended Peg's sense of order. Therefore, while Monica was hoping for a response like "absolutely maam, he is in room 814. You can go right up and see him," what she actually got from Peg Burrows, fan of organization and politeness, was "wait in line maam, just like everyone else."

This did not sit well with Monica Anderson. This was the perfect time for Monica. This was definitely not a good time for Ellen. Ellen would have moved to the back of the line. No, actually Ellen would not have moved to the back of the line. Ellen would have begun at the back of the line. In fact, if someone had then entered the waiting area and had looked like they were in any way ill, Ellen would have said, "go ahead. You can go ahead of me. I'm just looking for my boyfriend, who has a number of things wrong with him. But you obviously have something wrong with you, so you go ahead of me. Its fine, I'll wait." So, luckily for everyone involved, well everyone except Peg and the other patients. Well actually, I guess it was only lucky for Monica and Ellen; Monica was there, not Ellen. It is difficult to understand, I know. At first, I had a hard time coming to terms with it as well. Best not to think about it, just let it roll.

"Back of the line? I don't think so lady. My best friends boyfriend has been missing for several hours now. He is a narcoleptic, an epileptic, a hemophiliac and a diabetic. Do you have any idea of the various scenarios that may have befallen him during the last several hours? If he fell into a dialepticnarcophiliacal seizure while shopping for steak knives and spatulas, she needs to see him. And I'm not going to stand here, waiting in line when you can type in H-E-R-M-A-N D-O-U-G-L-A-S into your little computer and then hit F9, or whatever the hell you have to hit that makes your computer look for him in this god forsaken hellhole, and just fine him. So type it in, hit F9 and then I'm out of your hair. Otherwise, I'm going to stand in front of you, letting you know how much I hate you, until you do."

Peg Burrows had never been spoken to like this. She had been spoken to in a number of ways, not all of them positive, but when it was all said and done, no one had ever spoken to her in this way. So, she did hit a button. But unfortunately for Ellen Duncan and Monica Anderson, as well as for Dilbert Douglas and August Feducialiter (Dr. Wilkes had suggested to Dilbert that if he wanted to he might want to give himself a last name. Dilbert, surfing the internet they had provided for him in his room to help cure his boredom had come across the ancient Latin word Feducialiter, which means confidently, and had decided, with confidence I might add, that Feducialiter was a wonderful last name), that button was not F9 to search for Dilbert Douglas, but instead Peg Burrows hit the button that makes security come pick up crazy people from the front desk. And with the grace and fragility of the Bubonic Plague, Ellen Duncan and Monica Anderson were escorted to a beautiful little room with a small barred window and no sharp instruments. While Monica had committed herself to helping Ellen find her wonderful boyfriend, the hospital had committed Monica for a battery of psychological tests to determine if she was crazy or just super rude. During the initial intake period, they took a look at Monica's wallet and found that her identification all had a picture of her but the name Ellen Duncan. When they asked who Ellen Duncan was, Monica told them that Ellen Duncan was her best friend, and the reason for her coming to this hospital. She was looking for Ellen's boyfriend when the horrible hag at the reception desk had decided to send her to the funny farm. The doctors determined that while some of her statements might be somewhat true, Monica Anderson, who they attempted to call Ellen Duncan with little success, was in fact crazy. When you think about it, she was crazy. But at the same time she was incredibly successful. She held down a job. Well, Ellen held down a job. Monica was rather lazy. Ellen was a waitress at a restaurant called Lou's. Lou's was a lot different than Michael's, but not so different. Lou's was like taking Michael's food and dipping it in grease. Michael's was like taking Lou's food and dipping it in pretentiousness. Monica was a writer. She had not yet written anything, but she believed that she was possibly the greatest author in the history of time. She just had to come up with a story.

 Dr. Wilkes thought it would be best for August to stay in the hospital until they figured out who he was. They had contacted the police and no one had a missing persons out on him. Honestly, the only person who really knew he was missing was just down the hall really. So they thought that the best thing to do was keep him there until they figured out who he was. Interestingly enough, Dr. Wilkes was a student of psychiatric medicine. This was in fact the reason he was still August Feducialiter's physician. He could have easily passed the case off to an intern, but he was fascinated. He was equally fascinated with a story that one of his peers, Dr. Cody, had told him about that very day. A patient came storming into the hospital looking for her friend's boyfriend. She actually had a split personality and was actually apparently looking for her own boyfriend. So, after taking a look at August, Dr. Wilkes made his way seven doors down to Ellen Duncan's room where he met a lovely young woman who assured him that her name was not Ellen Duncan. Ellen Duncan was her best friend. Her name was Monica Anderson. She was Ellen Duncan's best friend. Dr. Wilkes decided to try to gleam some information from her, to get her to answer some questions that they typically ask of individuals with split personalities.

"Tell me Monica, do you remember what you were doing earlier today?"

"Yeah, I was trying to find Ellen's boyfriend. She was really upset and she asked me to go find him."

"Ok, but do you remember what you were doing before that?"

"I was working on my book."

"What kind of book?"

"It's a novel. I am a novelist."

"Oh, well that's very interesting. Have you ever had anything published?"

It was at this point that Monica got somewhat upset. Ellen was always harping on her about the fact that she could not call herself a novelist until she had published a novel. It made sense to Monica, much like wearing a helmet when riding a bicycle made sense to Monica, but Monica did not wear a helmet when she rode a bicycle and she had not been published, but that did not mean that she wasn't a novelist, much in the way that not wearing a helmet does not mean that Monica is not a cyclist.

"Publishing a novel is not the key to being a novelist. The key to being a novelist is writing a novel. When a tree falls in the forest and no one is around to hear it, it still makes a sound, and when I write a novel and no one publishes it, I am still a novelist and that is still a novel. Tell me Dr. Wilkes, when you are at home, not getting paid to be a doctor, are you still a doctor?"

"I see your point Monica. You are a novelist and I am a doctor. It is what we are, without outside intervention. So, how many novels have you written?"

As you well know by this point, Monica Anderson had never written a single novel. Monica was like a fireman in the ocean. She was like an ice salesman in the Arctic. She had no product, another fact that Ellen was quick to point out to her on a regular basis. And now, here was another person who was going to say exactly the same thing.

"Dr. Wilkes, are there any particular procedures you have never actually practiced, but believe you could do if you had to?"

"Yes Monica, I would say there are a few procedures I could do despite never having done so. But I am not sure what that has to do with my previous question."

"Well, there are some procedures I have not yet followed through with, but I know how to do them. I have not yet written my masterpiece. I need my story. I will find my story and I will write my story and then I will have my novel. But this does not not make me a novelist."

"Alright, so how do you pay for rent?"

"I don't pay for rent, I live with my parents. They pay for everything."

"Well, that's nice. What do your parents do?"

"My father is a lawyer and my mother is a stay at home mom."

Dr. Wilkes was very interested. Few splits had a good back-story, nor did they have a lot of details about their lives. Monica was somewhat of an anomaly, and at this point Dr. Wilkes decided that their conversation was done for the day. He retired to his office to document the two very interesting cases he was currently working on. Meanwhile, August Feducialiter sat reading a newspaper, hoping some article would grab his attention and jog his memory. Monica Anderson was sitting at the bedside table, pen and paper in hand, trying to write a masterpiece, with no real idea of what that masterpiece would possibly be about. There were options, but she didn't know that.

While Monica Anderson sat in her room, attempting to write her great masterpiece, putting together the pieces of her great masterpiece, or at least trying to, August Feducialiter sat in his room, doing much the same, except instead of his masterpiece, he was trying to piece together his life. It was much the same thing as Monica was going through, but unfortunately, if she didn't like the story she could simply change it. She could start again without any concern for what would happen. But in August's case, he had to have the right story. If he had the wrong story, he could end up on a plane to Guatemala. What if he thought he was in fact a Guatemalan dress manufacturer, or even a Swedish meatball taste tester? He could think he was an African prince and end up in the middle of the Sahara. It was unlikely that he was an African prince, given his whiteness. It was unlikely that he was Swedish because he had jet-black hair. It was unlikely that he was Guatemalan because he was mostly speaking English rather than Spanish, or whatever they speak in Guatemala. So, he was back at square one.

August began to contemplate his situation, trying to consider all his options, trying to figure out who he was. If it were you, how would you figure out who you were? I would probably put my picture on TV, hoping my mom, or girlfriend or some other caring individual would recognize me and come rescue me. August thought very similarly. And he asked the doctor to put his picture up on the television. Dr. Wilkes thought this was a good idea, so they took a picture of him, and asked the local channels to put it on the evening news. While we continue to learn the story of August Feducialiter, just imagine a possible issue with putting his face on the news.

Dr. Wilkes thought that one very important aspect of getting August back into normal life was getting him talking to people. So, he asked August if he would like to meet some other patients, some other people who were in the hospital. August also thought that this would be a wonderful idea. He was excited about the prospect of meeting people other than Dr. Wilkes and this was a good opportunity. Dr. Wilkes had a great idea. Here he was with two patients, one who did not have any idea who he was, and one who thought she was somebody else. True, it was like a weird game, playing with people's minds and emotions, almost using them as though they were toys. But, it was also really entertaining. It was like putting two scorpions in a small box and seeing which one came out alive. In this case, as a practicing physician, he wanted both of them to come out alive. But he also wanted to see what would happen. Obviously, now that August was interested in hanging out with some other people, he had to check with Monica to see if she would be interested.

"Monica, I was wondering if you would like to meet some other patients?"

"Why?"

"Well, I just thought, if you're going to be here, you might want to spend some time with some other people. There are some very interesting people around here. In fact, there is one person that I would like you to meet that is very interesting. In fact, he might be an interesting person to write your novel about." It was much like telling a small child that there was candy in the room that you wanted them to go into. They would go into that room, looking for the candy. Now that Monica knew where the candy was, she was clearly going into that room.

"Well, I guess that might be all right. I mean, I suppose I could use some of my down time and meet some people. I suppose that might be alright."

"Great, we'll head down to the recreation room and you guys can get to know each other."

Dr. Wilkes led Monica Anderson down the hall and into the recreation room. He sat her down in a comfortable brown corduroy chair facing the television. While she watched the Today Show and contemplated the absolute failure of Al Roker. Seriously, Al Roker is a failure. He may seem successful. He is a well-known and popular weatDilbert. He has a great number of fans. People love him. People thoroughly enjoyed watching Al Roker. But he was still a failure. Why was he a failure? Because he was fat. Fat people were failures, as far as Monica was concerned. Monica was herself, not fat, nor was Ellen Duncan, August Feducialiter or Dilbert Douglas. Speaking of August Feducialiter, he now entered the room, accompanied by Dr. Wilkes. The two made their way towards Monica.

"Monica, this is August. August this is Monica." Dr. Wilkes stood by the two new friends as they began the normal introduction methods. However, August had no idea what the normal introduction methods and Monica was confused as to what the hell August was doing. He began by trying to shake the same hand that Monica outstretched. As Monica outstretched her left hand, August outstretched his right hand. This meant that they could not possibly shake hands. And it is difficult to explain to someone who is not a four year old how to shake hands without laughing at them. And when you laugh at someone and they don't find it funny, that makes them angry. So, the relationship between Monica and August began poorly.

August took a seat a few feet from Monica. Monica stayed seated a few feet from August. August pretended to watch The Today Show, starring the great Al Roker, of whom, despite never having seen before, August was a big fan. Monica sat observing August. One of the keys to being a great writer, a great novelist, is to be observant. Monica Anderson was observant. She watched August watching Al Roker. August was a fairly good looking young man. In fact, August was beautiful. She was suddenly observant of the fact that August was wonderfully attractive. August was an attractive young man and one interesting fact about Monica Anderson was that she quickly developed crushes and one interesting fact about August Feducialiter was that he was an attractive young man. True, he obviously had no idea that Al Roker was fat and hideously untalented. But, he was attractive.

Meanwhile, August was considering specifically different issues. He was concerned about a cold front moving up the east coast. Of course, August was not entirely sure which coast he was on, or if he was on a coast, or what coasts they were talking about.

"Hey, where are we?"

"I don't know how to tell you this August, but we're in a hospital."

"I'm aware that we are in a hospital Monica. What I meant was, where are we geographically. I'm not an idiot."

"Do you realize that you are saying you're NOT and idiot because you don't have a sweet clue what part of the United Stated you are in?

I mean, it would be less idiotic if you knew you were on the east coast, just outside metropolitan Boston, but were unsure that you were in a hospital."

This was another instance where it could have gone either way. August could have leapt from his seat, grabbed the remote control from the chair side table and smashed Monica repeatedly in the face with it, screaming, 'shut up you blithering whore'. August could have taken the pencil, which she was using to make notes for her novel, that was being held in Monica's left hand, and stabbed it through her jugular, pulling it out to watch the blood shoot from her neck. But, he did neither of these things. Although, when you think about it, this would have likely been the perfect place to do either of them. If he smashed her in the face, there was a plastic surgeon a hundred feet away. If he stabbed her in the jugular, there was probably some doctor who could put her all back together again. Really, if there was one place where Monica Anderson would be perfectly safe despite a myriad of physical attacks perpetrated against her, it was there at the hospital. But August was not angry at Monica's comments. In fact, he found it pretty funny. In fact, he found it hilarious, and this was the first thing that he had found funny, ever, technically. Technically, August had never found anything funny ever in his entire life and now that he found something funny he laughed. He laughed a deep, hearty laugh and he continued laughing for quite some time.

Monica thought that this was extraordinarily amusing. In addition, as the beautiful young man named August Feducialiter laughed and laughed, Monica Anderson began to fall into what she felt was love with August Feducialiter. She moved her seat a few feet closer to August.

"So, why are you here August? What's wrong with you?"

"Well, that is interesting. I have no idea who I am. I mean, technically my name is not August Feducialiter."

"What do you mean? What's your name then?"

"I don't know what my name is. I literally don't know what the hell is going on. Here I am in the hospital with no clue what's going on or where I live, or what I do for a job, or if I have family, or if I have a wife, although I don't have a ring so I don't think that I have a wife, but I could have kids. I mean, I can't imagine me having a lot of children. But I could have some children. I could have one or two children, likely from a brief relationship with the girl I took to prom, assuming I took a girl to prom. Hell, I could have taken a guy to prom. I could absolutely be a homosexual. I don't think that I am a homosexual, but I could be." In fact, one of the reasons that August was rather sure of his heterosexuality was that he found Monica Anderson very attractive. She was gorgeous. She reminded him of someone in the back of his mind, but he brushed that thought aside so that he could concentrate on her. Monica, meanwhile, was busy taking notes, trying to determine if a) this handsome young man who called himself August Feducialiter would make a good character for her novel, b) if August Feducialiter might possibly gain the privilege of making sweet love to Monica by the fire and c) if Al Roker really was that fat or television just added the extra weight. Oddly enough, each of these held a 33.3% repeating amount of importance in her current life, giving you a good idea of the sort of heinous fragility that Monica Anderson suffered from.

"So, we're outside Boston? Alright, that's a good start. I don't suppose you know who I am, or where I live."

"Unfortunately, I do not know you, nor do I know where you live. I know where I live, but I do not know where you live. Maybe you live near where I live. Do you live anywhere near the market on Young Street perhaps?" Monica did not wait for an answer. "Of course, you don't have a clue where you live, so there's no real reason for you to know the answer to that question. Do you know anything about your life? I mean, what is your favorite color?"

"I don't know what my favorite color is."

"Maybe you should try to figure that out. I mean, knowing your favorite color is an important part of life. We need to figure out what your favorite color is."

"How do you figure out what your favorite color is? Can you just pick a color and decide that's your favorite color? How does that work exactly?"

"I'm not sure how you pick your favorite color. I mean, I know my favorite color is blue, but I don't know how I came up with that. I think you just need to experience colors and you will figure it out. Let's start by looking around this room and figuring it out from there."

The unfortunate part of this was that they were in a hospital. For those of you who have never been in a hospital, the color choices are minimal. For example, if it turned out that August's favorite color was taupe, or beige, or off-white or even eggshell, he would have been set. Hospitals don't want to get anyone worked up. They want to keep people calm and relaxed. The last thing you want in a hospital is a room filled with orange and purple polka dots. So, in a hospital, unless your favorite color was crème, you were unlikely to find inspiration on this particular quest. In this case, August's favorite color was orange and there was no orange in the hospital. True, there were shades of orange in the hospital but August liked orange orange. He didn't like off-orange and semi-orange or even white mixed with a minute amount of orange. And since he didn't like off-orange, he was not going to find his favorite color in the hospital. But since he didn't have any idea what his favorite color was, he thought it might be eggshell.

August began to get hungry. All this thought of eggs and crème and oranges was stimulating his hunger. He did not know why but he had a craving for something sweet.

"Do you have anything to eat? I am starving."

"All I have is this Crispy Crunch bar. Do you want that?"

August did want the Crispy Crunch bar. He also wanted Monica. So, he found a fine balance. "Well, I don't want to eat your whole chocolate bar, why don't we share it?"

The two somewhat unique individuals sat down and shared a chocolate bar. Monica felt happy because she shared a chocolate bar with this extremely handsome young man that she was beginning to fall madly in love with. August felt happy for two reasons. Firstly, Monica was a very pretty young woman and August enjoyed sharing the chocolate bar with her. As she devoured the very phallic chocolate treat, August remembered something that excited him but he could not remember what it was. There was something very exciting about her taking the chocolate treat in her mouth. Secondly, August felt a sudden rush of joy as he ate the chocolate treat. This joy turned to a euphoric rush and this euphoric rush was a result of his diabetes. The sugar rushed through his body. It built up in his system like so many times he didn't remember before. He got a feeling that would have felt familiar because he had had it so many times before. But it was not familiar, because to August, it was the very first time he had ever felt this sensation. As such, he was unaware that he should seek medical attention. As such, August fell to the floor in a minor diabetic coma. Monica screamed for help. Right before August fell into this coma, he looked up and saw a familiar face. It had been a long time since he had seen a familiar face. As he attempted to sound out her name, the only thing that came out was L. L was all he could say, and this meant nothing to Monica, Ellen's best friend.

When August came to, he did not know who August Feducialiter was. He also didn't know who Monica Anderson, Ellen Duncan or Dilbert Douglas were. He had no idea who he was, where he was, or why he was here. He thought he was likely in a hospital due to all the wires and plugs attached to him. He did not believe he was the six million dollar man and thus he did not believe that he was in some sort of ultra-secret military facility where he was being turned into some sort of crime fighting super hero.

"August, how are you feeling?" asked Dr. Wilkes, who the man in the hospital bed had not noticed.

"I'm sorry, what was that?"

"I asked how you were feeling. You passed out in a common area. You had a little more sugar than a diabetic should and slipped into a coma. We were lucky that you came out quickly."

"And did you say my name was August?"

"Well, sort of. When you first came here a few days ago, you didn't know your own name. So, since its August, I thought that was a good first name and then you decided that Feducialiter would be a solid last name. Since that point, we've been referring to you as August Feducialiter. Do you remember anything?"

"Not really. Not at all actually. How long have I been in here?"

"Well, you were here for about two days. You woke up the first day, and we ran a couple of tests on you. Then you went to sleep and when you woke up, you didn't even remember the tests. So, we pretended to run them again, just to see if it would jog your memory. It didn't. So, you went to hang out with a friend, who was unaware that you have diabetes. She gave you a half a chocolate bar and then you woke up here."

"I have a friend here in the hospital? That's weird isn't it?"

"Well, actually, she's another patient of mine. She was interested in your case because she's a writer so I introduced the two of you and you seemed to get along very well."

"This may seem like an odd question but, is she hot?"

Dr. Wilkes began laughing. He laughed and laughed. August thought, 'great. I'm sure she has a very nice personality with extra wide birthing hips. She probably has ridiculous snaggleteeth and collects pocket lint.'

"Monica is a very attractive young woman."

"Then why are you laughing?"

"You have to understand August, that when you first came in, a few days ago, I was astounded at how calm you were. You, an individual with no memory of who you were or where you were from, or anything of that sort, were seemingly unconcerned with the entire proceedings. Now, as you awake from a diabetic coma, as I tell you that we have no idea who you are, where you are from, who your family is or what your life is all about, the only thing you seem concerned about is whether your new friend, whom as far as you know, you've never met, is hot. To me, that is mildly amusing."

August considered this. It did seem rather entertaining, perhaps out rightly amusing and he decided to allow himself a chuckle. So August Feducialiter chuckled. Dr. Wilkes chuckled with him. The two chuckled.

Not far down the hall, Monica Anderson was not chuckling. She had finally found a lovely, handsome man whom she felt at ease with, a man who was well mannered and polite, and, as has previously been mentioned, rather handsome and she had nearly killed that man with a

Crispy Crunch. This did not make her chuckle. In fact, it made her cry just a smidge. Her best friend had a great boyfriend who was sweet and kind and wonderful and she had no one. Soon, they would get married, start a family and she would be left behind. She needed someone. She needed August Feducialiter. So, she did not chuckle.

Dr. Wilkes went back to his office and began working up the case files for both August Feducialiter and Monica Anderson. These would be the things of medical journals. It was rare to come across a true amnesiac, one that was not merely suffering from some sort of post-traumatic stress syndrome. It was equally rare to come across a coherent, non-violent split personality. And putting the two together in a room, if only just to see what would happen, was wildly entertaining. These would be the things of medical journals and Dr. Wilkes was a man who was very interested in being in medical journals. Medical journals got you research grants, extra money, cars, and a variety of other perks. And Dr. Wilkes was a man who liked perks.

August Feducialiter was a man who knew nothing of perks. He knew nothing of cars, research grants or extra money. August Feducialiter was a man of simple means, mostly because he was unaware of what complex means were. He was a man who was concerned with things like his name, his favorite color, his allergies, his dreams and his favorite sport. Suddenly, August became suddenly and extremely aware of the desire to know what his favorite sport was. It might seem like a small matter, but what are most important are your favorites. 'What is my favorite sport,' thought August? He knew the sports. He knew what golf was, he knew what soccer was, he knew what football was and he knew what hockey was. But he did not know which was his favorite. So he thought he might take a look at the TV and see if anything tickled his fancy, unaware that few men of his age used the term 'tickle my fancy' anymore.

Turning the television on, August began to flip channels. He flipped through cooking shows, talks shows, and soap operas. He flipped through news shows and through children's cartoons, and then he flipped back to the news show. He took a look in the mirror, and then back at the television, then back at the mirror, then backs at the television. Yes, he was on the television, this was clear. Just down the hall, Monica Anderson saw him as well. She turned up the volume to hear what the reporter was saying.

"A local hospital is asking for your help this evening in identifying a young man found unconscious at a local restaurant. The young man is unable to remember anything about his life and if anyone has any information about who this young man might be, or has any information about him whatsoever they are encouraged to contact the local police department who will follow up on that information."

Monica Anderson began to consider a very awful thought for her. 'What if they found him? What if he lived somewhere far away? What if he was from Texas? What if he was from Thailand? What if he was the king of a tribe in Africa? What if he was the king of Denmark? What if he had a queen? Of course he had a queen. He had to have a queen. He was beautiful. He was kind and sweet. It was then that Monica Anderson decided something that would seem at best, unethical, or at worst, despicable. No one would ever find August. She would ensure that no one found him. He would be her king, her Thai lover, her cowboy, her August. She became disinterested in the idea that he might have someone who cared for him, someone who needed him, someone who wanted him. He had to be hers. He had to be. She would ensure that no one find him. She would bury him. No one would ever find him. She would make it work. And they would live happily ever after.'

Not too far away, someone else was watching the same news report; August. August somewhat different take on the entire thing. 'What if I live far away? What if I am from Nevada? What if I'm from Korea? What if I am a small Maori tribe in New Zealand? What if I am the king of Spain? What if I eat humble pie? What if I have a queen? Oh my god. What if I have a queen? That would be fantastic. I might have a queen. Why wouldn't I have a queen? I saw myself on TV. I'm damned handsome. I am a beautiful, kind and sweet man and I obviously have a deliciously beautiful queen waiting for me at home at my palace. I absolutely must be found. I must ensure that I am found and that my queen knows where I am. And we will live happily ever after. It's official, I am going to find my queen and live happily ever after.'

Dr. Wilkes sat in his office watching the news and had his own take on the entire situation. 'What if he is amazingly important? What if he is the heir to a huge medical company? What if he is the son of an important doctor? If these were true, than by finding his family Dr. Wilkes would ensure that he would be rewarded. This reward would likely be an amazing new car, a larger office, a position with their world-renowned pharmaceutical company, or perhaps he could even marry into the family, eventually taking over the family business.' As such, Dr. Wilkes must ensure that August Feducialiter's family was found.

August made his way down to his 'friend' Monica's room, following the directions that Dr. Wilkes had given him and entered her room.

"Hello August," said Monica upon seeing him entering the room, seemingly confused.

"Hello, Monica. Your name is Monica, right?"

"Yes August, my name is Monica. I can't believe you don't remember me at all, after the times we've shared."

"Haven't we only known each other for like a day?"

"Well, it's true that we have only 'known' each other for an extremely brief period of time, I feel as though we have shared so much."

"That's true I suppose. I hear we shared a chocolate bar and you almost killed me."

"I did not mean to kill you August. I didn't know you were a diabetic and if I had have known you were a diabetic; we would have shared a cracker instead. I just wanted to share something with you. I still do."

August, remembering slightly what it was like to be hit on, blushed just a bit. He remembered what it was like to be the prey of a woman, and he remembered how wonderful it was to in fact be caught. Although he was searching for his queen, August thought it would not be so bad to delay himself by getting to know his subjects a little better. And how could his queen possibly be mad at him. He didn't even know he had a queen. Clearly this was not his fault and he would tell his queen so when he saw her again.

"Well, that sounds lovely. Would you like to share a walk with me for now?"

"Absolutely."

The two mentally unstable patients made their way through the halls of the hospital, Monica paying attention to August's every word, August paying careful attention to every turn to try to remember how to get back to his room. As they walked, they talked. They conversed. August got to learn a lot about Monica and Monica got to learn very little about August. But she liked what she did learn. She liked it a lot. August learned that Monica was a novelist working on her first novel. What was it about? She wasn't sure. She really didn't know. But she was working on it. What was his favorite food? Not sure. In fact, he had no idea what kinds of foods he liked. Unfortunately he also didn't know what he was allergic to, so he would have to wait until the tests Dr. Wilkes was running on him came back. They were running tests to try to sort out his allergies so they could start him on a more rich and rewarding diet. Interesting. Very. What was her favorite color? Magenta. Definitely magenta. What color is magenta? Well, it's difficult to describe magenta, but my socks are magenta. Monica showed August her magenta socks and August now understood what magenta was. He was quite sure that magenta was not his favorite color. But it was all right. In fact, magenta might become his second favorite color. But not his first favorite. There was no room for magenta at the top.

"When will they have your tests back so we can start feeding you real food?"

"They said probably today sometime."

"Well, why don't we go down to the cafeteria and see what they are serving today. Then we could take a look once the tests come back and figure out what we'll be eating on our first date."

Oblivious to the connotations suggested by Monica, August thought this would be a good idea. "Yeah, that sounds great." Monica thought this would be a great idea.

Dr. Wilkes returned home to his family for the day. He decided that a day off was in order. So, he drove the 23.7 miles from the hospital to his lovely three-storey house in the suburbs. Robert Wilkes lived at 23 Juliet Avenue, one of many unfortunately named streets in the 'Shakespeare' area of the suburbs. Some of the other possible streets Robert Wilkes could have lived on were Romeo Court, Titus Road, Hamlet Street or Othello Lane. When it all came down to it, Robert Wilkes felt extremely lucky that he lived on Juliet Avenue. After all, it could be worse. 23 Juliet Avenue looked eerily similar to 25 Juliet Avenue, located just to 23's right. It also looked eerily similar to 21 Juliet Avenue, located just to 23's left. In fact, almost every single house on Juliet Avenue looked eerily similar to every other house on Juliet Avenue. One contractor had been hired to make Juliet Avenue look like the most beautiful neighborhood in all of Verona. However, this had its' own issues as well.

Juliet Avenue and its' eerily similar houses had resulted in no less than two divorces and no less than two assault charges. For example, returning home from work one day, Jacob Carlisle had driven into the driveway of 44 Juliet Avenue instead of 46. This would not have been a huge problem if it were not for the fact that his wife was purposely at 44 Juliet Avenue, 'visiting' a neighbor. This was divorce number one. Divorce number two was eerily similar to divorce number one except that when Mark Fielding sent flowers to his lover's house, 19 Juliet Avenue, they were actually delivered to 39 Juliet Avenue, his own home. Mrs. Diana Fielding thought that it was sweet that her husband would send her a dozen red roses but was uncomfortable with the note that read, 'tonight will be even better than last night, Love Mark', because her husband had been at a Boy Scout's meeting the night before. The assault charges need not be explained. They stemmed from similar situations. Almost every married man on Juliet Avenue had now placed some sort of marker at their homes in order to ensure that they remained married.

Robert Wilkes did not need to place any such marker at his home. He was an honest man and was also unmarried. He returned home to his dog, Fletch. Fletch was a 10 year old Chocolate Lab that welcomed home Robert with a deep, hearty bark and a slobbering kiss. This was fine by Robert who loved Fletch very much. He walked from his front door into his kitchen and made himself a sandwich. Ham, mayo and bread all came together in a beautiful union of sandwichocity. He washed down his sandwich masterpiece with a large glass of orange juice. It was fulfilling and refreshing. It was delicious and emotional. It was a ham sandwich and a glass of orange juice. Meanwhile, Fletch ate small brown kibbles, sorting through his bowl of food as to avoid bits. But he did like the kibbles. Robert settled into the living room onto his black, faux-leather couch and turned on his 42" flat screen television. Normally, Robert would turn to either ESPN to check the scores or one of the various local channels to see whether 'Rodrigo' had returned from the dead or if 'Thad' and 'Kelsie' would get married, despite interference from his mother, 'Tabitha'. Soap operas were one of Robert Wilkes few vices. Soap Operas, hot dogs and pornography. These were Robert Wilkes' vices. Today however, Robert's attention was drawn to local news. The local news had all picked up the story of August Feducialiter, whom they had dubbed 'The Summer Man', and were launching regular stories asking for help in identifying him. No one had come forth thus far. No one seemed to know who August Feducialiter was. Robert was concerned that the love of his life might remain his Chocolate Lab Fletch and that he might never marry August's sister and take over the Feducialiter family business. Fletch gave Robert another kiss and Robert was dismayed.

It was Fiesta Day at the hospital cafeteria which meant that as long as August was not allergic to corn, chili powder, hamburger and tomato sauce, they would be able to take their pick of 'South of the Border' delights. Monica, herself a fan of Mexican cuisine, suggested that enchiladas or tacos would be a wonderful choice, in combination with 'Mexican fries', a horrible concoction invented by the genius marketing team at Taco Bell. Someone decided, and it turned out to be highly successful, that along with making a mockery of the traditional foods, fries should be covered with a cheese-like substance. Monica, brought up on imitation Mexican food, loved 'Mexican fries'. She felt that if there were one reason she should make the long trek to Mexico someday, it was to enjoy the thrill of having 'authentic Mexican fries', not knowing that 'authentic' or 'traditional Mexican fries' were invented at the Taco Bell district offices in Liverpool, New York. 'Authentic Mexican food' was closer than they thought.

As they returned to August's room, luckily for August Monica was with him because otherwise he definitely would have gotten lost, Dr. Sloan met them there. Dr. Sloan was one of Dr. Wilkes' partners and was responsible for filling in for Wilkes while he was taking the rest of the day off. He informed August, in an extremely doctorly way, that while August would have to be very careful with his sugar intake, he did not suffer from any major food allergies. While corn might cause some discomfort a few hours later, this was a normal suffering of most of the human race. So, August and Monica made their way to the cafeteria where August believed they had their first meal as best friends and Monica believed they had their first date. It was a lovely time and August discovered that while he liked Mexican food, he did not believe that it was his favorite. It might come in second. It likely would not slip as far as third, because he did enjoy it. But it would not likely be his favorite. There just did not seem to be room at the top for Mexican food.

Three hours later, August Feducialiter decided that not only was Mexican food not his favorite, but it was slipping further and further down the food chain if you will. If it were not already the case that he were hospitalized, August felt that this food could have hospitalized him. August had a private room and it was at this juncture that he realized that this was good, because if he were sharing a room with someone, his roommate would not likely be friendly with him anymore. August wanted to make sure, considering his delicate condition, that he did not make this same mistake again. And it was due to this first unfortunate meeting with Mexican 'cuisine' that the August diary came into existence.

Chapter One: Things that make me feel bad. 1. Mexican food. Mexican food will make me feel like I am shooting a water gun out of my rear and will create an odor that I can only assume is the worst smell in the history of time. 2. Sugar will in fact kill me. I should not eat sugar unless I want to die. Also, some things that you would not think have sugar, do. Wine has sugar. Candy has sugar. Rum has sugar. Fruit has sugar. All these things will in fact kill me. If I feel like I might die, see a physician.

Chapter Two: Things that make me feel good. 1. Monica. Monica is pretty. And she is nice. And she is pretty. I think she likes me. She looks at me funny and when she does I sort of feel funny. I might have a queen and if so, I need to be careful with Monica, because I think she wants a piece of my kingdom. 2. Silly Putty. As the name suggests, this is a very silly thing. But it is a lot of fun. It is NOT edible. It has a very plastic flavor to it. In fact, this entry should later be added to Chapter One, because while playing with Silly Putty makes me feel good, eating Silly Putty makes me feel bad.

Chapter Three: People I Know. This is a short chapter, but it is extremely important. 1. Monica. As per my previous entry, Monica is nice and pretty and I like her. She is a novelist working on her first novel. I think she might be writing a novel about me. She takes a lot of notes while we are talking. 2. Dr. Wilkes. He is a nice man. He asks a lot of questions and seems pretty amused by me. I like him. 3. Dr. Sloan. Dr. Sloan is kind of boring but also really nice. He told me about my allergies and about what I can and can't eat. 4. Andrea. Andrea works in the cafeteria. She is really nice and she gave us all our food for free. (August was unaware that as a patient, he was provided his food for free.) I will make more entries as I meet more people. Oh. 5. August Feducialiter. That's me, sort of.

Just a few rooms away, Monica was doing some writing of her own. She was making notes on her novel, tentatively called "An August to Remember." The title was kind of cheesy, but maybe that was the kind of novelist that Monica Anderson was. She was not sure yet. She could be a John Irving, or a Stephen King, or perhaps even an Adolfo Bioy Casares. She did not know who she was. Of course, she felt bad making a statement like this because she was working on writing about a man who REALLY didn't know who he was. At least she knew that she was Monica Anderson and not anyone else. So, he didn't know who he was. Well, in Monica' story, he was an important young man. He was the eldest son of a wealthy oil tycoon from West Texas. His family was searching for him with all their resources. But, he was under the radar, being cared for in a Guatemalan prison hospital, after a plane crash that killed a priest when the plane crashed into the local church. As the only survivor, August was being held captive, responsible for the entire debacle. His family were searching all through the United States, unaware that he had been traveling to South America on a trip to see his fiancée, who was a doctor, working to cure AIDS in South America. Had they known this, they would have gone looking for him there. BUT, they didn't even know he was engaged. He was engaged in secret because his fiancée's parents were sworn enemies of the Feducialiter's. It was like Romeo and Juliet. In fact, it might be too much like Romeo and Juliet. No, it was an oft-copied story, which she would resurrect in the greatest love story since… Romeo and Juliet. Except he would not stay with his fiancée. He would fall in love with the beautiful nurse who was taking care of him while he could not remember who he was. Yes. THIS was going to be her first novel and it was going to be the greatest love story of ANY generation. Yes. It was her time to shine.

Monica was curious as to what Ellen was doing right now. She must be worried. Monica usually checked in with her at least once every day or two. The silly fools at the hospital were refusing to let her go home, insisting something was wrong with her. She felt fine. She felt fantastic. She actually felt better than usual. But these idiots were refusing to believe her. Of course, there were certain things that she was enjoying while she was here. There was the wonderful food. If every day were Fiesta Day she might never want to leave. She was writing again, or more to the point, she was writing for the first time. While she did consider herself a novelist, she had not in point of fact ever written a novel, nor had she succeeded in writing a draft. She had not as of yet made any notes on possible novels. She had not written a synopsis. She had not drawn a small stick figure cartoon that outlined the story she would like to write. She had not written anything until she had met August. August had inspired her to write and for that she owed him. And she loved him, so there was that too.

Ellen was a wonderful friend, which is why Monica had agreed to go find Dilbert for her. While it was true that it had been a somewhat monumental failure, she had at least offered to go look for Dilbert. Albeit, she had not found him, and had herself been remitted into the custody of the state until medical officials had cleared her for release. It was a little strange that Ellen had not come looking for her yet. But she was probably extremely busy at work. So, it was not that surprising. It was fine. She was not even concerned at all.

'Why is no one looking for me?' thought August. 'We have confirmed that I am likely super important. I am devilishly handsome. I am witty and kind. I am a catch. So why is it that no one seems to be interested in catching me?' August was quite surprised. But then he thought that they might just be busy. I mean, as the head of a multinational crime syndicate and or oil empire, his father would be very busy with business and/or murder and/or extortion and/or all of the above. His mother would of course be on vacation in the Dominican where she was likely sleeping with a young man named Raoul. Raoul was a handsome young bartender who was probably only sleeping with Mrs. Feducialiter for her money, but for Penelope Feducialiter, it was money well spent. His siblings would rather he not be found. With August out of the way, they would be free to fight amongst each other for the family fortune. So, it was not that odd that the family was not out looking for him. It was fine. He was not concerned at all.

Robert Wilkes was beginning to become concerned about the fact that no one appeared to be looking for August. His face was plastered all over the news, in every police station in the city and CNN had agreed to begin covering the story to some extent. It was an interesting personal interest piece. People seemed to like personal interest pieces. It was as though they were interested in them, as people. The local news was in fact sending a reporter up to the hospital to interview August. Robert had thought it was a brilliant idea. Hopefully it would lead to August being recovered by his family and Robert would be richly rewarded. They would obviously come looking for August. There was nothing to be concerned about. It was fine. He was not concerned at all.

August decided to take a walk to clear his head. Not that his head was particularly full. I suppose it was full of questions. But there was a definitive lack of answers. A head full of questions might as well be considered empty. But he decided to clear his head nonetheless. He wrote down his room number in his newly created diary and took the diary with him. He figured that it would be best to have something to go by, and right now that diary was all he had. Sure he had a friend in Monica and a sort-of friend in Dr. Wilkes. But neither of these could be with him right now, so he brought the diary instead. The diary told him the things that made him happy, the things that made him unhappy and the people he knew. The last item on this list was very short. But he thought he would make a solid effort at adding to that list while he was on his walk. He walked up to the nurse's station and introduced himself.

"Hello, my name is August Feducialiter. I'm a patient of Dr. Wilkes'."

The first nurse to answer August's greeting was Amanda Bale. "Hello August, it's a pleasure to meet you. My name is Amanda. I'm one of the nurses who was helping you when you first came in. You probably don't remember me."

"Well, I don't. But don't feel bad. I don't remember me either." August laughed, a deep laugh that filled his chest and rolled out into the nurse's station like waves over the rocks when the tide rolls in and Amanda smiled. It was a wide smile, set around a full and bright set of white teeth. Her smile was like a sunrise, full of joy. And then Amanda laughed. She had a deep, throaty, genuine laugh, like that sound a dog makes just before it throws up. But sexy-like. She was clearly attractive. August could tell that. It was at this point that August remembered. No, that's not the right word. He didn't remember that he liked women, he just knew that he liked women. He felt that he liked women, and he sort of felt like he liked Amanda. Whether he recalled it from some old Renaissance movie that he had seen or whether he invented it all by himself, August took Amanda's hand in his, kissed it very gently just between the knuckles and said, "it's a pleasure to meet you." August remembered how to flirt. Or maybe flirting is a natural response. Maybe flirting is like the Babinski reflex. Maybe flirting is like breathing. You don't remember or forget how to breathe, you just know. And August just knew how to flirt. He really didn't want to forget Amanda, because then he would have to learn all over again that he was incredibly attracted to her. So he wrote her down in his book.

Chapter Four: Amanda The Beautiful. Amanda is the nurse who helped me when I first came in to the hospital. She has short brown hair and I think she looks like a movie star. She has baby blue eyes that ask me questions that I really would like to answer and she has a deep laugh that is an odd combination of sexy and revolting, but more sexy than revolting. Her favorite food is…

"What's your favorite food?"

Her favorite food is pizza, specifically Hawaiian, partially because she loves pineapple and partially because she has never been to Hawaii, but would really like to. She wears a pink nurses uniform. I think it's a nurse's uniform because all the other nurses seem to be wearing the same thing. Its entirely possible they just all happen to have similar taste in clothing, but it seemed more likely that this was the uniform. Her favorite color is…

"What's your favorite color?"

Her favorite color is brown. It's her favorite because it is no one else's favorite that she has ever met. In the history of time, it is entirely possible that brown is no one else's favorite color. It is entirely possible that since someone said, 'let there be light', no one in the entire world has ever liked the color brown. And it is very soothing. Brown might be my new favorite color, but for Amanda's sake, to ensure that she is still the only person in the history of time whose favorite color is brown, I shall not choose it as my favorite. She grew up in outside Detroit and moved here when she was eleven with her mother, after her parents got divorced. And she is shockingly beautiful.

August made his notes in his diary while Amanda stood there, stupefied by the behavior of the handsome, quirky young man standing before her. She did not ask what he was writing. She got the idea from the questions that he was asking that he was taking notes. For someone who could not remember anyone, it seemed like an appropriate use of time and resources.

"Well Amanda. It has been wonderful to meet you, but I must be moving on. It is a large hospital and there are a great number of people

I would like to meet today. But will you be here tomorrow?"

"I will August. I work from 3pm-3am."

"Well, then I hope I will get to see you tomorrow."

"I look forward to it as well."

August left the nurses station and made his way through the hospital. He made his way to the cafeteria. While it seemed odd, especially on the day when he was looking to meet new people, but August felt that need to see a familiar face. He was hoping that Andrea would be working still. He found that she was not, but Mike was. So, he introduced himself.

"Hello Mike, my name is August. I don't have a very good memory, I'm a diabetic and I don't care for Mexican food."

"Well, hello August. My name is Mike, I'm a Scorpio, I enjoy long walks on the beach and I have to get to work. If you have an order, great. If not, thanks for coming out."

August took out his notebook and made a new entry. Chapter Five: Mike from the cafeteria is a prick. Mike kind of seems like a prick. He is sarcastic and rude and made little or no attempt to make friends with me when I tried to make friends with him. Therefore, Mike is a prick and I will not be attempting to hang out with him anymore. Instead, I shall wait for Andrea to return. Andrea is not a prick.

August made his way back up to his room, amazed that he was able to do so with such little effort. As a queuing system, August drew a map of the hospital, as he had seen it thus far but on his way back to his room he did not once have to refer to it, which was good because he was a terrible artist. He sat in his bed, thinking about the two people he had met today. There was Amanda. Amanda was light, and lovely, and beautiful and kind. She was a good friend. Then there was Mike. Mike had bad acne, and he was fat, and his facial hair was crooked and he was a prick. Thus far, August had determined that he liked women more than he liked men. He liked them more as friends and he liked them more in the way that his pants became tighter suddenly. He had first noticed this tightening of his pants and coinciding butterflies in his stomach when he met Monica. He decided to see if Monica still caused the pants tightening and stomach flying so he stopped by her room. He had also drawn a map to her room.

"Hey sweetie. How are you?" Monica was genuinely excited to see August. Firstly, she was working on the notes for her book and she could always use more inspiration. Secondly, she missed him. When August wasn't around now, she felt like she wanted him around. She had never really had someone, except Ellen of course, that she missed. She had never had someone that she wanted to be around that much. But now she did. August made her feel good. He made her feel wanted. He made her feel special. And not many people had ever made her feel special. But August made her feel special so she was more than happy when he made his way into her room.

I'm ok. I've been exploring today, meeting new people and exploring the hospital. It was fun."

"Well good. Have you eaten yet? We could go have our second date."

Once more oblivious to the connotations, August agreed to his second date with Monica without ever really realizing that he had gone on his first date with Monica. She suggested that they once more frequent their favorite restaurant, the hospital cafeteria. Given the limited options set before them, he agreed, as long as that dick Mike wasn't working. Monica asked who Mike was and August informed her that he was a dick who worked in the cafeteria.

"Well, even if that 'dick' is working, we shouldn't let that ruin our time. We can still have a nice time."

August assured her that he would try.

The two friends made their way through the maze of taupe and crème walls, eventually ending up at the cafeteria. Monica had her arm linked with August's, enjoying the feeling of connectedness that this particular position afforded her. August did not mind. It actually felt rather comfortable, and he too had gone too long without physical contact. They entered the cafeteria and were greeted not by Mike, the dick, but by Andrea, the sweetheart.

"And how are you two doing this lovely day?" asked Andrea the sweetheart.

"Quite well," replied August. "Much better now that you are here. I had an unfortunate run-in with one of your co-workers earlier today."

"Ahhh. You met Mike I assume."

"Yeah. He's sort of... well, he was just kind of..."

"He's a dick. Always has been always will be. I don't know why. No one knows why. He just is, and you have to take him with a grain of salt. Now, what would you two like to sample this evening?"

"What are the specials today mademoiselle?" inquired Monica.

"Well, we have a lovely cheeseburger, made with perfectly aged beef and a smooth slice of American cheddar. That particular meal comes with the fries au curl, but you can substitute for a side garden salad, which consists of about three pieces of lettuce, a sliced carrot and four pieces of cucumber. That also comes with your choice of fountain drinks."

"Oh that sounds quite nice," observed Monica.

"It's delicious. We also have a very nice ham sandwich. Several thick and juicy slices of ham, layered on two pieces of white bread. The sandwich is topped off with a wonderful mayonnaise. This also comes with your choice of potato, as long as your choice of potato is curly fries. You can also substitute the fries for a lovely garden salad, but given my description of the garden salad, I would go with the curly fries."

"I think that sounds very nice. I don't know why but I feel as though I would like the ham sandwich." August was unaware that he did truly love ham sandwiches. He had unknowingly eaten ham sandwiches for a very long time now.

"The ham sandwich is another lovely choice, but there is one more option. We also have a pasta casserole. It is a wonderful medley of macaroni showered with a selection of two different cheeses. (We ran out of cheddar so we made half and half with mozza). It is a healthy portion of macaroni and comes with your choice of homemade white roll or a tea biscuit."

"Hmm. I think I'll have the macaroni and cheese casserole. How is the tea biscuit?" asked Monica.

"It's like a small beige hockey puck."

"Well then. I will go with the roll."

"Excellent choice madam. And for the gentleman?"

"I think I am going to go with the cheeseburger with a side of fries au curl."

"Wonderful sir, and to drink?"

"Do you have any champagne? This is the one day anniversary of our first date," said Monica, trying to romanticize the moment just a little more.

"We do not, but I do have a very nice Sierra Mist. It's very similar."

"That sounds excellent."

"And for the gentleman, might I recommend a beer of the root variety?"

"You are a magnificent waitress Andrea. That sounds absolutely perfect."

"Great, well why don't the two of you have a seat. When your meals are ready, I will bring them to you."

The two friends, now on their second date, made their way to their favorite of the twenty banquet tables that lined the hall that acted as the hospital's cafeteria. Small talk was a difficult task for August due to his lack of knowledge of anything locally, regionally or nationally relevant. For example, political debate was virtually impossible. August was unaware how a president was elected, who the current president was or even that the United States had a president. So, political conversations were right out. Sports talk was limited. August had seen a very brief smattering of highlights, but nothing that would allow him to really carry on a conversation about sports. Monica was a skier. She loved to ski. August said that sounded really nice. Then Monica explained what skiing actually involved and August said that sounded really nice. She told August about the time that she had caught an edge, flipped end over end a few times, slammed into a tree and broke her arm. August said that that did not sound very nice.

"Why would someone do something that could result in something like that?"

It was then that Monica realized that August would like being a golfer, or a ping-pong player, or maybe a pool player, but that a career in football, hockey or even tennis was probably a little 'rough' for his gentle demeanor. She hesitated to use the term pussy, but it did pop into her mind.

Weather was a topic that August was very interested in. He didn't remember ever having been outside so he was curious as to what it was like.

"Oh my god. That's right. You've never been outside. Well, you've been outside, but as far as you know, you've never been outside. Well, after our dinner, we need to go outside."

"I don't think we're allowed to leave the hospital."

"We can get a doctor to go with us maybe."

"Yeah, that might be nice."

"It will be beyond nice. It will be magnificent. It's just so weird to think of all the things you've never done, or seen, or felt. Do you remember snow?"

"I know what snow is. But I can't remember ever having seen or felt snow. It's the white stuff, right?"

This blew Monica's mind. The whole concept of not knowing anything about anything, of having lived a life without remembering any of those experiences, was absolutely surreal. Yes, that was the word. It was surreal.

"Yes silly, it's the white stuff. Do you remember the first time you ever kissed a girl?"

August had to stop and consider this. He knew, of course, what a kiss was. The union of two sets of lips, the moistness, the heat. He remembered it all. Or rather, he had an idea about it all. But he could not for the life of him remember ever having kissed someone. He did have a fleeting memory of his mother kissing him on the forehead before bed, but he doubted this was the sort of kiss that Monica was referring to. She meant a real kiss. A real kiss, as he saw it, was a paradox. It was sharp and soft. It was warm and cool. It was sweet and lightening. It was a whole collection of things that didn't make sense with one another, which was possibly the reason that it was so powerful. August felt like he had kissed someone before, but he had no evidence to back this up. He could not envision the face that he had kissed. He could not remember the lips or the tongue or any portion of the face. So, it was possible that he may have never kissed anyone. But he thought that he had.

"I don't really remember ever having kissed a girl. I think I have but I can't remember."

Monica walked towards him, slowly and purposefully. She walked with the look of an animal stalking its prey. This was the first time that August took a look at her entire body. This was the first time that he ever noticed her hips. To this point, he had barely glanced below her chin, but now he soaked up her entire being. Her hips jutted out just enough that you could tell where they where. He knew where her hips were before his hands settled on them. They snapped from side to side with a certain fluidity. And when his hands came to rest on them, their motion was stopped. He could smell her. It was a sweet combination of roses and cinnamon. It was possible that these were the result of perfume and chewing gum, but it smelled, no, it felt, as though it came from her very core. It felt as though the center of her being was made of bits of roses and cinnamon.

It was at this time that August realized that Monica had every intention of kissing him. He had a short period of time in which to make a very important and difficult decision. Would he kiss her? There were a number of considerations in this decision. Firstly, did he believe that he had a queen waiting for him elsewhere? And if so, did anything that he did while not "himself" count against him? Did he get a "get out of jail free" card for not remembering who he was? Also, did he like her more than he liked Amanda? If not, it would be unfair to her to kiss her. It is not often in one's life that one discovers that they have two distinct choices of women. It is even rarer that someone who has no idea who they are would have two beautiful young women interested in him. But, this seemed to be the case.

His choices were suddenly and irreversibly removed from consideration when Monica took the opportunity to kiss August. It was very sudden. August was not sure what to do, but that quickly sorted itself out. Her lower lip caressed his upper lip as though it were an ice cream cone. Not wanting to devour it to quickly, it simply tasted it. The kiss then made its way deeper in. Her tongue began to taste his upper lip, as her lower lip had done just before. It delved deeper and found his tongue, which had by this point decided it would like to become involved and met its counterpart with the most imperceptible pressure. The two tasted each other in this most intimate of ways and then, similar to the manner in which they had come together, quickly and without warning, they came undone.

Monica, upon breaking August's "first kiss" turned and walked out of the room, leaving August to ponder what had just happened. Upon pondering what had just taken place, August was left with a few conclusions. 1. Kissing is really nice. His first kiss had been very nice and he hoped that future kisses would be equally nice. He could not even fathom the idea that kisses could be better than this. 2. He was definitely attracted to Monica. It was not just because she kissed him, although that didn't hurt. There was something about her. She reminded him of someone but shockingly, he couldn't seem to recall who. 3. Did he love her? Maybe. Maybe not. He barely knew what love was. It was more than just a feeling, that tightening of the pants he had previously felt. Love was something wholly new to August, if it was there at all. All this thinking, this loving, this kissing, caused August to get tired. For any normal person, this would not be a major concern. But, in a narcoleptic like August's case, it became a major concern. In fact, it became more than just a major concern. August began to slip. August began to fall. He began to drift into a narcoleptic snooze. And as he went from standing, to slouching, to kneeling, to laying he began to remember. He remembered the first time he ever kissed a girl and that girl was not Monica. He remembered his first time eating a cheeseburger and it was not with Monica. He remembered going for walks in the snow and none of those walks involved Monica. In fact, none of his memories involved Monica. I mean, he didn't call her Monica. But she looked just like Monica. It was as though he were looking at Monica's twin. He remembered kissing her, but her name was not Monica. It was Ellen. Her name was Ellen. That's right. His girlfriend's name was Ellen. He grabbed his diary as he was drifting away and wrote one half sentence;

"My girlfriend's name is…"

Monica's walk back to her own room was less confusing, but no less interesting. She knew that she was in love with August and no one else.

She was enthralled with him, and her kiss confirmed it. Her kiss confirmed that she loved him and she believed it confirmed that he loved her. She knew that she had no other. She knew that he was the only one for her. She knew who she was. And she knew who August was. He was the love of her life and she decided to make her way back to his room and tell him so. She walked briskly down the hall, not making the same motions with her hips that she had made in August's room. That had been for his benefit, not hers.

As she walked into the room, she was surprised and concerned to find August lying on the floor. He seemed to be sleeping peacefully so she was not that concerned. She was going to wake him, and then she thought she should probably call a nurse. She called the nurse and then noticed his open diary. She looked down at it and her heart dropped. She read that one line and her heart fell. She picked up the notebook and placed it on his desk just as the nurse entered.

"What happened?" asked the nurse, attempting to surmise the reason for her patient's slumber.

"I don't know. I came into his room and found him this way."

"He'll be fine sweetie. He's just sleeping. Would you mind helping me get him up into his bed?"

The two lifted August up onto the bed. They placed his blankets around him and propped his head up with a pillow.

"I have to do some rounds. Are you ok staying with him for a little bit?"

"Of course. I'll take care of him."

"Great. He's lucky to have a friend like you."

The nurse left and Monica sat down beside August. She read over the line written in the notebook over and over again. She read it and thought, 'what else could it mean?' It could have meant virtually anything. It could have been that he was thinking of Monica and also of the Oscar Meyer wiener song. Maybe he remembered the song but was actually unaware that he remembered the song and believed instead that he was writing a sweet and caring love song for his NEW girlfriend, Monica. Maybe that's what he meant. Hell, maybe he didn't even write it. Maybe someone else wrote this, and August was so shocked that someone would desecrate his notebook in this manner that he actually had an epileptic seizure, born of rage. Perhaps it caused him to pass out in anger, and he had of yet been unable to recover from it. How could she possibly figure out a way around this? Hmmm. Well, it was probably best to finish his sentence. So, Monica wrote her name down at the end of the sentence in August's notebook. "My girlfriend's name is… Monica."

When August woke up, he found his best friend, his girlfriend even, sitting by his side.

"Hey sweetie. How are you feeling?"

"Umm. I feel ok." Obviously there were certain aspects of August's reawakening that were not ok. For example, August didn't have any idea who this woman, sitting beside his bed, was. He didn't know where he was or why he was in this place. He also didn't know what the date was, what the month, season, or year was. He also didn't know who he was. He didn't know what his name was. He didn't know where he was from. He didn't know what his favorite color was and he didn't know if he was an only child or one of seventeen children. He may have been the Prince of Spain, or he may have been the starting tackle for the Green Bay Packers. However, one of the problems with all of this was that he did not know where Spain was or that Spain used a monarchy, at least as a figurehead system. In addition, he didn't know who the Green Bay Packers were, what sport they played, what positions there were on a football team and what each of those individuals did. But he didn't want to seem confused, so he replied. "I feel great. How are you?"

Monica could not help but laugh. "I'm good. But you don't have any idea who I am do you?"

"It's not that I don't know who you are. I don't know who anyone is."

"Well, that's why you've been keeping a diary, to make sure you know what's going on. Maybe you could read over it to get an idea who everyone is and what's going on."

And with this, August took the time to read over his diary, getting a good sense who everyone was. He was very interested to find out that he had a girlfriend. He would have to find out who this Monica woman was. "So… you are…?"

"I'm Monica. You may have read about me in your book."

"I did. You're my girlfriend."

"It's true." And with that, Monica leaned into her 'boyfriend' and gave him their second, first kiss. It was magical. It was delicious. It was wonderful and fantastic. It gave August a feeling of tightness around the groinal region of his pants. He liked the feeling of tightness around the groinal region of his pants. It gave him butterflies in his stomach, and he also enjoyed this.

"So, how long have we been together?"

"Well, let's see. It's been so long. We've been seeing each other for about three days. We sort of made it official yesterday. Before that it was just sort of a casual thing, seeing each other in the halls or wherever. Hanging out in the cafeteria and such."

"Very interesting." What August meant when he said 'very interesting' was, 'WHAT? What the fuck are you supposed to say to that? I don't have any idea who this chick is. I like to kiss her. I like to look at her breasts through her flimsy hospital shirt. I enjoy her company, well, what I know of it thus far. But she's my girlfriend and I have never seen her before. The book does seem like something I would write. It appears to be written in my 'voice', if such a thing exists But still, this is the weirdest and creepiest thing that has ever happened'. August smiled at his girlfriend and told her he needed to use the washroom.

As he stood in front of the porcelain urine receptacle, holding onto the only thing that seemed even remotely familiar to him, although it seemed smaller than he remembered, August contemplated what was happening. Sure, he had been told that this woman was his girlfriend. And sure, she was pretty enough that he wasn't complaining about it, but it still seemed a little weird, a little odd, a little surreal if you will. He had never really met this woman but now she was his girlfriend. All right, he decided, better make the best of it. He finished with a couple of shakes(more than two and its considered masturbation) and returned to the room where his girlfriend was waiting for him.

"So, its not that I'm complaining. I want to make that clear first off. I am definitely not complaining. You are extremely beautiful. You seem smart, and funny and wonderful. It's just that I don't know you.

I'd like to know you. I'm not saying I'm not committed to you. I just need some time to sort this all out."

"Well, this is one of the problems we have. Every time that you fall asleep, or pass out, you forget everything. That's why you started your diary, so that you'd have a way to know what was what."

"Right."

The doctor broke through this momentary awkward silence by entering the room and telling August that they had to give him some insulin.

"Sounds fantastic. And that's for?" August was certainly fine with taking whatever the doctors told him, but he was at the very least curious about what it was for.

"You're a diabetic August. It means that your body can't control its sugar levels without our help. Its especially important that if you ever feel overly tired, or the opposite, overly euphoric, you let us know so that we can monitor and adjust your insulin levels."

"Don't worry doctor, I'll take good care of August." Monica was committed to this relationship and felt that the role of nurse might be one well suited to her demeanor.

"Good. Its good to have friends in a situation like this." The doctor was amazed. Sure, it was great for the two of them to be getting along so nicely. But when an amnesiac and a crazy person begin a relationship, you have to assume that things are likely not what they appear to beon the surface.

"Listen, there is a small room on this floor that we thought you two might want to use to watch a movie or something. You know, take some time to get to know each other." The doctor was actually, to say the least, amused. Sure, he might be somewhat sadistic in this manner, he might be just doing this because its entertaining, but he was still helping take care of them at the same time, so I guess it could be forgiven.

"Do you wanna watch a movie August?"

"Sure. I've never actually seen one before, so that might be nice."

I can't count the number of times that I have tried to pick a movie out to watch with a couple of people only to find that it is absolutely impossible to agree on a movie to watch. Imagine now instead that you were trying to pick a movie with someone who had never seen a movie, didn't know what a movie was, had no sweet clue who their favorite actor is, didn't know if they liked comedies or dramas or horrors or action flicks. Imagine if the choice of what to watch was entirely up to you. It was basically a matter of just picking whatever movie you wanted to watch, while attempting to reconcile that choice with the wants and needs of someone who has no idea what their wants and needs are.

The other issue with this particular date was the choice of films. Aside from personal collections, most of the films that the hospital had in its possession were not exactly the type of movie you curl up with each other to. For example, I have never curled up and made out during *The Land Before Time Part 4*. I have never gotten head from a girl while we watched *Chicken Run*. I did once get head while watching the 1990's animated version of Spiderman, but that is an entirely different story and one that I do not plan on sharing at this time. So the choices that were given were as follows; The Iron Giant, The Lion King, Pinocchio, Toy Story, Toy Story II, Rocky III, and Miami Vice. The latter two were actually the personal possessions of Dr. Jake DiRossi, a third year student from Ohio who had moved her to be with his girlfriend Jennifer. He didn't actually tell his girlfriend that he was coming to Boston. He didn't mention to her that he would be coming to her house at precisely 7:28pm. He didn't tell her that he would sneak delicately into her home. He didn't tell her that he would have a dozen roses or that he would make his way almost silently up the stairs to the first door on the right, which was of course, her bedroom. Some things that Jennifer never told Jake were as follows; I will be dressed in a school girl outfit, I will have my hair in pigtails and finally, and most importantly, I will be fucking Dr. Nicholas Kazperzak. This was of course, for Jake, a very WTF moment. He actually said, WTF, only he did not use the abbreviated form. As Jennifer balanced herself between fear, guilt and the delicate throes of an orgasm, she realized that her relationship with Dr. Jake DiRossi was likely over. Jake realized that he was going to find his own place in Boston. Nicholas Kazperzak didn't really realize anything except that he was likely not going to get to finish.

Monica and August sat in beige recliners that smelled like old people and amoxicillin and watched Toy Story. About forty-five minutes in, August fell asleep for a couple of quick nods so they had to start the whole thing from scratch again. Between that and a small break to eat and ensure that August's sugar levels were okay, the whole ordeal, which is not what you want to hear a third? date called, took around three hours. Following the date, the two made their way back to August's room where they made out. It was glorious and fantastic. Both had a wonderful time. Then, August felt like he was getting a little tired, so the two called it a night and August forgot who Monica was... again.

It was at this point that Monica began to question her relationship with August. She wasn't questioning how she felt about him, or how he felt about her. There was no question that the two cared for each other. The real question was whether the relationship could really last. I mean, informing your boyfriend every single day that you are his girlfriend is just balls out annoying. It would be a frustrating way to spend your time, but you would still be with someone. She had never really been with someone and felt that the slightly annoying need to constantly inform your partner that he is in fact your partner, was nothing when compared with the warm body in its place. So, questioning, yes. Giving up, not quite.

The next day, the two decided, after Monica told him who he was, and what his relationship to her was, that they would go on another date. No progress had been made on the front of trying to find August's family and things seemed grim. So, they thought that it was a good idea to have some lunch and then maybe watch a movie. Dr. DiRossi thought it might be nice for them to get out of the hospital for a date and having lots of money given the fact that he was a doctor and had no girlfriend to speak of, Jake decided that he would treat them to dinner. Andrea had been expecting the two in the cafetorium and went to find out where they were. Mike, the huge prick who also worked in the cafetorium, was working anyways; Andrea just liked to be around to help out the cute couple. She came across them on their way out.

"Hey kids. I expected to see you in the caf today. It's 'Tastes of the World Week' and today is Hungarian Goulash and French Fries."

"Sorry Andrea, Dr. DiRossi asked us to go out for dinner and while the cafetorium does have some wonderful food, we thought it might be nice to get out of this place for the night." Monica thought that it was a wonderful idea; August was just a tad bit scared of the possibilities.

"Oh, that does sound like a very nice night. Well you kids enjoy you. Hopefully you'll be back soon. We have a whole week of worldly delicacies, sort of." Even Andrea had to laugh at the idea of comparing the cafetorium food to delicacies in any way, shape or form. Nonetheless, it made her laugh.

"Would you care to join us?" asked Jake.

Andrea's attention suddenly switched from the two star crossed lovers to the devilishly handsome doctor standing before her. She decided that it might not be a bad idea to spend some quality time outside the hospital and outside her busy knitting schedule. Since her divorce, almost 2 years before, she had spent the majority of her time practicing her knitting abilities.

"Well, I would not want to impose. I mean, is your wife going doctor. I would hate to be a fifth wheel."

"There is no wife. So, you would not be a fifth wheel."

"Well, in that case, I would be happy to join you. I'm Andrea."

"And I am Jake," said the handsome young doctor, offering his hand out towards the attractive young cafetorium worker. The two shook hands slowly, with purpose. He, feeling the delicate softness of the spot between her thumb and index finger, she feeling the firm strength in his handshake. The two of them were testing each other, tasting each other and so far they both enjoyed it.

"HELLO!!!" Earth to you two," hollered Monica, interrupting the moment with her own subtle brand of joy.

"Sorry. Let's get going. My car is just parked around back here," replied Jake, suddenly returning to his senses.

The four made their way to the back of the hospital, piled into Dr. Jake DiRossi's brand new BMW and drove across town to a lovely little Italian restaurant called Colaicovo's. It had reasonably good food at a reasonably good price and Jake thought it tasted just like home, which for him, in the most primal of concepts, was Italy. Over the course of some scrumptious Greek salads, which is really weird to have in an Italian restaurant, a combination of various pastas in a plethora of sauces involving pestos, meats, and vegetables, some cheesecake and 2 magnificent bottles of Colli Altotiberini, the four really got to know each other, sort of. Well, Jake got to know Andrea, and August got to know Monica, and Andrea got to know Jake, but there was little to know about August and Jake and Andrea didn't bother really filling August in knowing full well that August would not remember any of this just a few short hours from then. And so they focused on each other.

Jake discovered that Andrea was quite pretty, pretty attractive, attractively quiet, and quietly horny. He discovered this as she worked her foot up and down the inside and outside of his thigh. Andrea discovered that Jake was very rich, richly humorous, humorously handsome and handsomely horny. She could tell this because he said, "so, when this is all over, where would you like to go" and he winked. So the two decided that when they were all finished with supper, and after dropping off August and Monica at the hospital, they would go back to Jake's beautiful condominium and have another bottle or two of Colli Altotiberini, which was in fact Jake's favorite wine. Needless to say, the drive to the hospital was brief and purposeful.

"Thank you very much for supper Dr. DiRossi. It was lovely to be outside the hospital, even if it was only for a very brief period of time." Monica did indeed enjoy the supper very much and a date outside of the hospital with August was lovely.

"Please, it's Jake. And it was my pleasure. I had a wonderful time with you both and we should do it again sometime."

"Absolutely Jake. It was nice to get my mind off things. Not that my mind is on very much anyways, given my delicate position," August laughed, knowing laughter was a great escape and also the best medicine.

And with that, August went back to his room to contemplate his life as a man with a past, a history and no memory. Monica went back to her room to change into her other flimsy pale green dressing gown and then make her way to August's room to try to make out with him. Andrea made her way to Jake's thinking that she might soon be having her first sex since one extremely drunken, post divorce fling. Jake made his way back to his condo knowing full well that he would in fact be having sex with Andrea in no time. Finally, following an eventful evening for all, all slept. And August forget that evening and every preceding evening.

August awoke confused, requiring sugar, and with a slight hangover. Someindividuals might think it a little irresponsible to take a diabetic, narcoleptic, hemophiliac, amnesiac out drinking. One such individual who did think it irresponsible was Dr. Wilkes. As such the next day, Jake DiRossi found himself in Dr. Wilkes office.

"You took them out for DRINKS?"

"Well, I just thought that it was a good idea to get them out of the hospital for a little while, just for a change."

"It's a hospital Jake. It is not a resort. It is not a club. It is not Milwaukee. Sure, if this were Milwaukee, you might think that it would be a great idea to get out of town for a weekend. Maybe you could head to the Hamptons. But it's not Jake. It's a hospital Jake. They are our patients. We are their medical professionals. A couple of bottles of merlot and some pasta are not medical care. So, in future, when you think 'hey, this is a good idea' you should then think 'is this medicine or a date'. Clear?"

"I understand. I know it may not have been the greatest idea in the world, but they were with me the entire time. I was in complete control of the situation. I mean, nothing is really wrong with 'Monica'. And yes, things are wrong with August, but nothing that can't be controlled. Obviously, I'm not going to make this choice again, but I still don't think it was that bad of an idea."

One person who thought that it was a bad idea was August who was spending his morning in the washroom, getting rid of the contents of his stomach into the toilet following a night of heavy drinking, which he didn't remember, which is of course was a regular thing, for drinkers, and amnesiacs. All very confusing for everyone, drinkers and amnesiacs alike. Monica was making her way slowly down the hallway, sort of drifting back and forth as though she were, drunk and/or hungover. She made her way to August's room where she did not find him, visually, but she could hear him in the bathroom, spewing forth pesto, feta, linguini, garlic toast and wine. It looked disgusting. It smelled worse. And so, once August emerged from the porcelain receptacle, the two made their way to the television room where Monica catered to August's every need while August placed one foot on the floor in order to control the spins. There are a great number of mysteries and miracles in the world. How does gravity really work? How do they get the caramel in the Caramilk bar? Is there life somewhere else in the universe? But all of these miracles, all of these mysteries, pale in comparison to the mystery, the miracle that is controlling the spins. Lift leg, world spins at incredible speeds, making the spinee vomitously ill. Lower leg, all is right with the world. It just doesn't make any sense, and yet it is true, and beautiful and was currently saving August Feducialiter's life. August's diet for that morning consisted mostly of crackers, water and the contents and lining of his stomach. Monica's diet for that morning consisted mostly of lemon flavored water and an orange-banana-bran muffin. The muffin gave her an unfortunate case of diarrhea, which she explained to a clueless August, meant uncontrollable pooping. It is interesting, and in fact uniquely insightful to judge someone by the verbiage they use concerning genitalia, bodily functions and mating habits. For example, Jake told his friend that he fucked this chick that worked at the hospital named Andrea. Bold, crass and to the point. While Jake is a fairly nice man, this description of his intimacies lends us to believe that he might not be quite as nice as he would have us believe. Andrea on the other hand, who told her best friend that she slept with a gorgeous doctor who she worked with at the hospital and that he had an extremely large, but still nice, 'you know' was clearly a more delicate individual than Jake was. This is not an indictment of them as people, but instead it is merely a glimpse into their inner souls. Similarly, when Monica informed August that diarrhea was uncontrollable 'pooping', it spoke to her delicate nature, her simple childishness. Meanwhile,

August had not felt comfortable enough with anyone yet to let his inner dirty self out to meet them. No one knew if he would say dick, or cock. No one knew if he would say shit, poop or crap and no one knew if he would say hump, fuck or screw. No one knew who he really was. Monica tried, but there is only so much you can know by looking at an individual who has never really looked at themselves.

There was a television in the common area in which they currently sat and on that television was Toy Story. August enjoyed the film. He had never seen it. Well, he had seen it. He had actually seen it recently. He had seen it two days previous. With Monica. Monica had seen the film a number of times. Most recently of course being just a few days previous. But she liked the film very much, and she wanted to see it again, so she decided not to tell August that he had already seen the movie. Hell, they might even watch it again that very day if he had a nap or a seizure. He enjoyed the movie. He really liked the part where Woody kept punching Buzz in the chest and Buzz's little button was getting pushed and he said 'Buzz, Buzz, Buzz... Lightyear to the rescue.' That was his favorite part. He spent the next several hours repeating that phrase. Monica began to wish that she had told him he already saw the movie, that he hated the movie, that the movie had made him violently and irrevocably ill. But she had not, and so this grown man, as they made their way through the hospital, kept repeating the same phrase over and over again. 'Buzz, Buzz, Buzz... Lightyear to the rescue.' It was annoying, but also cute, and so Monica let it continue, although it did at one point cross her mind that she should feed him several packets of sugar until he slipped into a diabetic coma, hopefully one he would quickly emerge from, minus the annoying Pixar quotation habit. Luckily, Monica's mind was just stable enough to consider this a bad idea. And so, August survived.

Mr. and Mrs. Nathanial Donald Douglas were vacationing in the south of France. While there, enjoying American money and French women, French wine and American cheddar, American films and French beaches, they thought little of their beautiful son. They did not think of the fact that Dilbert could not remember who he was. They did not think of the fact that Dilbert could easily slip into a diabetic coma.

They did not think of the fact that Dilbert could not play Nintendo or be in a community to poor to own a fancy new police car that didn't give people seizures because in either case, he could easily have a seizure. They didn't think about these things because of three equally unique and equally important reasons. ONE: They had left Dilbert in the seemingly capable hands of his seemingly sane girlfriend, Ellen. TWO: They constantly vacationed and nothing horribly ominous had ever happened previously. THREE: They were hammered drunk, in a delicate attempt to avoid the realization that they hated each other and would clearly get a divorce if they were not extremely drunk and amazingly careful. So, Nathanial Donald Douglas was busy getting his rocks off with formerly attractive, young women who had been in bars and clubs too long and refused to wear makeup, and refused to pay their tabs. Meanwhile, Elizabeth Diana Connors Douglas, was drinking so much wine that she was urinating merlot and cabernet sauvignon and had no idea what formerly wealthy, never attractive man she was currently sleeping with. Technically, they were staying at the Hotel Kepplar but this was nothing more than a launching pad for their blissful infidelities. So, the two did not think of their son Dilbert and his current predicament of which they were alcoholically unaware.

Similarly to Dilbert's parents, Ellen's parents were unaware of the situation that Ellen currently found herself in. Unlike Mr. and Mrs. Douglas, the Duncan's were not drunk. They were not in France. They were not sleeping with formerly beautiful, formerly wealthy people. They lived in a beautiful, calm, peaceful and safe town. Some of the accolades that town has won are as follows;

June, 1993: – Burlington rates as the best place in the nation for raising children in a report released by Zero Population Growth.

June, 1988: – Tied for first place as Most Liveable City by U.S. Conference of Mayors for populations under 100,000 (Portland, OR for larger cities.)

1996: – Burlington is one of America's Top 10 "Hippest Arts Towns," reports author John Villani in his new book, The 100 Best Small Arts Towns in America.

June, 1999: Ranked number one for "Families that love outdoor sports" by Outdoor Explorer magazine, premier issue.

These were just a few of the reasons that Mr. and Mrs. Duncan had decided to settle down in lovely Burlington, Vermont. They were as unaware of the fact that their daughter was a nut job as... their daughter was that she was a nut job. They were a little simple. They were living in a place voted one of the best places for raising children, but were no longer raising children. Sure, they were excited that they were living in one of the most liveable cities in America. They were not particular 'Hip Art' fans and they were not a family that loved outdoor sports. They were in fact lost. As a child, Craig Duncan vaguely remembered vacationing in a place called Burlington. He remembered it for its fantastic go karting. Craig Duncan loved go karts. And when it was decided that Ellen was old enough to fend for herself and the retired post office worker, along with his wife, the retired grade three teacher, decided that they wanted to move somewhere for retirement, Craig decided to pack up everything he owned, along with everything his wife owned and move to the greatest place for go karting her had ever seen. It was magnificent. It was a genius maneuver for a man who had spent his entire life mostly taking envelopes from one pile and placing them in another. It was an extremely wonderful and incredible idea, were it not for the fact that Burlington, Vermont does not have a single go kart track. Burlington, Prince Edward Island, Canada, does. Burlington, Prince Edward Island, Canada, has a wonderful go-karttrack; a mile long with some good straight-aways and some really great turns. Burlington, Vermont had a Magic Hat Festival. Burlington, Vermont had a quaint post office and two particularly wonderful coffee shops, where Craig spent most of his day, pining for go karting, and definitely not thinking that his daughter was a crazy woman who was living with an unstable man, in a hospital just outside Boston.

Dr. Wilkes began to believe that August's family was not looking for him. He began to fear that he would not be found. He began to fear that no one would ever come for him. He began to fear that he would not marry August's sister and would not become the heir to the family fortune, and as this thought shot through his mind, he began to consider that he might need to contemplate the long term needs of August Feducialiter. He began to think that he might need to consider the medical, emotional and psychological needs of August. He began to think that he might need to begin acting less like August's agent and more like August's doctor. And so Dr. Wilkes set out on a mission to make August better. Less than three hundred feet away, another individual very involved in August's life was thinking very similar thoughts. Monica was thinking that she needed to kickstart August's healing process. She decided to start with his physical well being and work her way down, or up, or around, from there.

"We are going for a hike," announced Monica as she bounded into August's room at 9:37am. This was startling for August, not because she bounded into the room and scared him and not because he was concerned about the hike itself, but rather, because August did not know this woman who burst into his room, or why he was in this room. Monica remembered this and led him down the now usual path of reading his diary, making any adjustments that she felt necessary and then finally kissing his now prickly face. After all this, August decided that he was in for the hike. He was in for pretty much anything. The thing that makes August (Dilbert) Feducialiter's (Douglas's) story possible is the ease with which he gave up any and all control of his life to others. Even before he lost the ability to sort out his own life without the use of diaries and second hand information, August was all-too willing to allow others to make up his mind for him, a trait that Monica had come to admire/abhor/love/hate about him. She loved that they got to do what she wanted to do. She loved that she got to decide when, and where, and how, and in most cases if. But she hated the constant weight that this necessity brought down upon her. Just once she wanted August to say that HE wanted spaghetti, or that HE wanted to watch Toy Story. But HE did not. August Feducialiter was a spectator of his own life and Monica resolved to change that. She resolved to make August at the very least a fan, and possibly even a participant.

"You need to exercise. Your body, your mind and your heart."
"And are you planning on helping me with each of these goals."
"I will absolutely help you with each of these goals."
"Well then I'm in."

"Good."

And with that, a pact was struck. Monica made him write it down so that he would not forget, or in this case, so that he could easily remember, or at least react to the details. August wrote it down. 'I, August Feducialiter, resolve on this day, the whatever day, of the whatever month of the whatever year, to begin anew, settling not for settling, but instead attempting to live life to its absolute fullest, and ensuring that no day is wasted.' Monica signed the pact as his official witness and then sealed the whole deal with a kiss.

Dr. Wilkes went looking for August at about the same time that Monica and August went looking for love in all the wrong places. He found the two on a park bench, just outside the hospital entrance. August's hand was perched precariously on Monica's left breast and his belt was undone. No real damage had been done, and yet Dr. Wilkes felt that he might have come at an extremely opportune time.

"Well, there you two are. I was worried about you. I thought maybe I could join you for supper today. The cafetorium is serving a delectable stir fry that I think you both might enjoy," offered up the doctor.

"Of course Dr. Wilkes. We would love it if you would join us for supper. Isn't that right August," replied Monica, hoping that August would say 'absolutely not. Stop talking for me as though I am a child you controlling sonufa bitch. For the love of all that is good, just let me talk for a minute and decide things for myself.'

"Yeah, whatever you guys want sounds good to me."

'FUCK,' screamed Monica in her head. She was beyond pissed that her boyfriend would not grow a pair and start living his own life instead of watching the made for TV movie version of it. "Great."

The three sat in the cafetorium, eating what they called a stir-fry. Apparently when you fry something and stir it, it automatically meets the requirements to be considered a stir-fry. It does not have to have any traditional ingredients; it doesn't have to have the right vegetables, spices, sauces, etc. This particular stir-fry was a combination of carrots, broccoli and strips of what was technically chicken. And yet, they still called it a stir-fry. And yet, it was not a stir-fry, because stir-fries are good and this was shite.

"August, how are you feeling lately," asked the good doctor?

"I feel pretty good. I mean, everybody's really nice, and I have Monica, which is pretty awesome."

"Excellent. Are you doing okay adjusting to everything?"

"Well, yeah. I guess so."

"Do you remember anything form before you were in here?"

"Not really. Most of the things that I 'remember', I get from my diary. I really don't have any idea who I am, but the diary has helped with that. So that's pretty good."

"And what do you want to do going forward?"

"What do you mean?"

"Well, do you want to get a job, or a place of your own to live? I can only assume you don't see yourself living in this hospital for any significant amount of time."

"I guess I never really thought about it."

"Well, maybe its something you should start looking at. I mean, its not that we don't want you around. But…"

"I guess I never really thought about it. I just sort of thought I'd remember everything at some point, and then live THAT life. I never really thought about what I would do if I didn't end up remembering."

"Well, maybe we should start planning for the idea that you might not actually regain your memory."

August had not previously thought of the idea that he would not regain his memory. He had sort of taken for granted the idea that he would someday remember who he was, where he lived and what he did. But now, he was suddenly inundated with the idea that he might not actually ever remember anything. It gave him a sudden sense of foreboding. It gave him a sudden sense of absolute fear for the future. And yet, he felt okay about the whole thing because at least he had a girlfriend who loved him and a doctor who cared for him. What he did not have was a sweet clue what he would do if any of these things did not work out for him. And this filled him with a foreboding sense of fear that started in his legs. It started in his feet. It felt as though his feet had gone to sleep and were now waking up, which felt very uncomfortable. It then moved his way up his legs, stopping at this thighs to make him feel as though he had worked out and was now feeling the burn. Then, the pain moved up into his chest and he felt as though he were having a heart attack. Then he had a heart attack. Luckily, the best place to have a heart attack is in a hospital, especially in the company of an experienced doctor. August was well cared for.

When Dilbert Douglas awoke, he felt awful. He had a headache. He had a great number of tubes attached to his body, along with a collection of wires and he could not imagine why he was hooked up to all this crap. But he was. And suddenly everything came back to him. He remembered all the times that he had not remembered who he was. He remembered Monica and then realized that Monica and Ellen were the exact same person. He remembered where he lived, and remembered what he did for a living and remembered where his girlfriend, Ellen, lived, which happened to be the same place that he lived, and remembered what she did for a living; she was a waitress. He remembered all of these things. He remembered that he was a diabetic. He remembered that he was a hemophiliac and upon turning the television on to MTV, which happened to be a strobe light dance-a-thon, he also remembered that he was an epileptic. However he remembered this just a tad bit too late. He remembered just a few seconds into his seizure and called out the one name that made him feel safe. The people within the rooms adjoining Dilbert Douglas' heard him call out that single name.

"ELLEN!!!"

And then he awoke again. This time, he did not know who he was. He did not know who anyone was, including himself. He did not know the myriad of diseases, syndromes or disabilities that he suffered from, nor did he know who Ellen was, or what issues from which she might be suffering, although to be fair, he actually didn't know that before he lost his memory, mind, etc. He awoke confused. He awoke with a headache. And he awoke frightened. He also awoke with a book by his side, which he decided to read over in case it might shed some light on everything he was seeing around him. And it did. There are in fact several new passages which I will now go over with you.

Chapter Six: Dinner with Dr. DiRossi. Dr. DiRossi is very nice. I think when he originally planned for this dinner, he was motivated by a desire to help me out. Once Andrea became a part of the whole thing,

I think he was more motivated by the need to fornicate. He and Andrea got along very nicely and I am pretty sure that following our double date they may have humped. Dinner was nice, I like Italian food. The wine was very delicious.

After these few sentences, possibly due to the very delicious wine, August's diary turns into a collection of misspelled words, unintelligible sentences and supremely confusing paragraphs. No one could have possibly understood the remainder of this chapter without a pair of prescription glasses that were not prescribed to the individual wearing them and six glasses of three fingers of really primo scotch. As such I will not attempt to burden you with that chicken scratch here, except to say that the more risqué of sentences in this passage dealt with his feelings for Monica. Apparently, while he would have fared poorly on a history test, he was actually pretty up to date with his sex ed.

Chapter Seven: Toy Story. This is a great movie. It's got love, action, excitement, and humor. It's got it all. It is a great movie and one that I will likely enjoy over and over again since I will never have any idea that I have previously seen it, nor will I object to watching it again. Actually, it might be interesting to see if I like it every time that I watch it. Stay tuned for future updates.

Chapter Eight: I definitely like Monica. A LOT. She is really actually even prettier than I thought before and she really likes me. I can only imagine what it would be like to, well, we'll leave that to the imagination for now. But she seems to really be looking out for me, and I think in my present situation, it would be a very good idea to have people around me who are looking out for me. Dr. Wilkes seems genuinely concerned for me, but he also has this look in his eyes when he is looking through his wallet, so, I am not entirely sure what is going on there.

This time, it was August who came bounding into Monica's room. Her room number was written by her name with a heart beside it and some directions on how to make his way from his room to her room. However, the entrance of August into the room still gave Monica somewhat of a start. Upon realizing who pranced into her room unannounced, she was less startled.

"And you must be Monica," the only logical thing to say when meeting your girlfriend for the 'I've lost count' time.

"I certainly am. And you are August, my loving, caring handsome boyfriend."

"Well, now that we have that sorted out, would you like to have lunch?"

"I would love to have lunch with you, dear."

The two made their way through the hospital, greeted along the way by several of their 'friends', until they finally made their way to the cafetorium. I don't know if I have mentioned this before, but I abhor the word cafetorium. I abhor the word for a variety of reasons. Firstly, it is stupid. There are two possible rooms. One is a cafeteria and one is an auditorium. Now, a cafeteria is a place for eating. According to an online etymology website that I referred to, the word cafeteria is a modern English word, stemming from Mexican Spanish. *Cafeteria* means "coffee store." The ending—*terrier* in this word came to be popularly understood as meaning "help-yourself" (as though *café +—teria* and was extended to new formation with that sense from c.1923. The word itself began its life in 1839). The other possible room, the auditorium, has a Latin root and is supposed to refer to a 'lecture room'. It can also be described as a 'place where something is heard'. It comes from the Latin *audire,* which means, 'to hear'. Now, I want you to truly consider the difference between these two words. One word means coffee shop and the other word means place to hear something. It is true that the reason for the development of the word 'cafetorium' is likely because certain institutions could not afford a coffee shop AND a place to hear something. So, they took these two ideas, these two rooms, and combined them into one. I have several arguments against this unholy union. First, you can fucking hear something in any room, anywhere. The idea of a special room solely for the purpose of being heard is a good idea. It is designed with comfortable seats, with an area from which people can speak, etc. The idea of combining this room with any other room is ludicrous and ridiculous. For example, when I build an institution, I am going to design a room called the shitatorium. This room will be for shitting and for listening. I suppose you could listen to someone shitting, but this does not seem to be the purpose of the cafetorium. Now unless you want to listen to someone buying, making or drinking coffee, scrap the one room insanity and build two frigging rooms. I mean, this particular hospital has a myriad of rooms which serve no practical purpose, but god forbid we have two rooms, one for eating and one for listening.

Nonetheless, the two made their way to this unholy of rooms and upon entering, were greeted with the warm smile of Andrea, their favorite cafetorium employee.

"Well look at you two lovebirds. Come down to visit your favorite of food preparatory workers," asked their favorite of food preparatory workers?

"We are indeed here to sample your fine culinary delight," replied the slightly more knowledgeable of the two friends. They were in fact there to sample Andrea's fine delights, in an entirely different manner than Jake DiRossi had sampled her fine delights, but they were there to sample them nonetheless.

"Excellent. And what can I whip up for you today?"

"I don't know. What do you feel like sweetie," asked Monica?

Of course, August had no idea what he felt like. He felt confused. He felt hungry. He felt like an opera singer who could not read music He felt like a college basketball player with very little in the way of hops. But he assumed that Monica was referring to what he felt like eating, so he kept all of that to himself and replied with a very simple, very expected "I dunno."

This infuriated Monica. It infuriated her in a way that she could not describe. It infuriated her in a way that made it difficult for her to breathe, to think, to move, to do absolutely anything. Andrea on the other hand was unphased by his inability to decide. Andrea could breathe, and did so. She could think, and did so. She could move and did so. She could do absolutely anything she felt like, which in this case involved trying to figure out what August might feel like, other than the ambassador to Spain.

"Well that's not a problem at all."

'YES IT IS!!!' screamed Monica inside her head, at the top of her lungs, inside her head.

"Here's what we're going to do. Mike is coming on shift in just a few minutes. You two may accompany me to the back where I will fix you the greatest meal that you have ever devoured," offered up Andrea.

The two lovers followed Andrea into the kitchen, past shelves stacked with chocolate milk, apples and small containers of green jell-o topped with what passes for whipped cream. They walked past small plastic trays filled with pasta salad and slightly larger trays filled with lettuce, incredibly hard croutons wrapped in plastic wrap, and little plastic thimblesque containers filled with fake Caesar Salad dressing, the kind that didn't use actual anchovie paste. They walked past shelves filled with cans of Coca-Cola and Dole orange juice. They entered the kitchen, which was actually quite spacious. Stainless steel appliances, purple and grey marble countertops and an endless supply of plastic gloves.

They made their way to the fridge and opened the flat, cold, steel door to reveal its contents to all who could see. There were pieces of meat, sliced into infinitely small pieces that would allow for maximum profit. There were pieces of cheese sliced so thin that they were transparent, also designed to maximize profitability. There were whole tomatoes, romaine hearts, loaves of thick whole wheat and white breads, bagels, endless jars of mayonnaise, several jars of mustard, three containers of ketchup and several large stackable plastic trays full of pre-cut potatoes, shaped into fries. Still, nothing jumped out at August, so Andrea began making some suggestions.

"Do you trust me August?" asked Andrea.

"Of course."

"Well good. Then why don't you sit back and relax and I will work my magic."

The key to a delicious fried egg sandwich is ensuring that you take delicate care in every aspect of the sandwich. For example, if the toast is too hard, it will ruin the sandwich. But we're getting ahead of ourselves here. A fried egg sandwich begins and ends with an egg. The egg should be a decent size, but not too large. And you want to use a fairly small pan. You don't want the egg to spread out too much. You want it to be just about the same size as the toast. Well, just a smidge larger actually. You want to make sure that the yolk is not too solid and not too runny. The last thing you want is yolk all over the place when you go to eat the sandwich, but at the same time, you want to enjoy the flavor. So, make sure the yolk is just a little bit liquid, mostly solid. Vegetables. Some people will tell you that you do not need vegetables on a fried egg sandwich. Egg purists would suggest you need egg, but I disagree. I prefer a fried egg sandwich made with one leaf of crisp, green lettuce. I prefer a fried egg sandwich with a firm tomato, with very little seeds. Too much seeds ruin the sandwich. You want most of the tomato to be the 'meat' with very little seed. Tomatoes have ruined their fair share of sandwiches, so be very careful. You want the egg to be golden brown. Too white and it is too gooey. You want the egg to be crisp. You want the egg to be firm. When you toast your bread, you want to make sure that it is toasted all the way through. Too many toasters toast just the center of the bread because that is where all the heat is. You want to evenly distribute the heat. If you were lucky enough to have a grill, this would be the ideal time to use it. Luckily, Andrea had a grill. And used it. So, make sure that the entire bread is toasted, just enough so that there are no white spots on the brown. That golden yellowy brown is what you are searching for when it comes to it. There are a number of side dishes, which act as good partners with the fried egg sandwich, but nothing seems to take the place of hash browns. Again, the key here is attention to detail. You need to be sure that the hash browns are the right size. Many a good corned beef hash has been ruined by overly large hash browns. Dice. Dice are the best way to think of hash browns. Anything larger than dice and you risk not cooking the potato all the way through, and you need to cook the potato all the way through. Otherwise, you risk eating overly browned potato and overly raw potato all in one fell swoop. Smaller than dice works, but are difficult to eat, depending on the size of your flatware. Spices can also make your hash browns successful or an absolute failure. Too much spice and you might as well just eat spices instead of spiced potatoes. Too little spices and the potato is too bland. I recommend some pepper, a pinch of salt, and a pinch of your spice of choice. Whatever that spice may be, use it sparingly. This, with a tall glass of orange juice will be one of the greatest meals in the history of time.

It was the best meal that August Feducialiter could remember. It was the only meal that August Feducialiter could remember, but to be fair to Andrea, it was also one of the best meals that Monica could remember, and she could remember quite a few more meals. It was magnificent. August copied the entire recipe down in his diary, thinking it possible that someday he might have to fend for himself on the food front.

"That was remarkable," exclaimed August to his chef.

"Well thank you August. I aim to please," just ask Jake.

The next hour or so was spent with small talk. This was difficult for August because of his lack of small, or big, knowledge about himself or the world around him. So instead, August played the role of secretary, recording some of what the two women said in his small journal. The journal filled up with half-caught conversations. There was a brief section on the recent romantic exploits of Andrea, involving one Dr. Jake DiRossi. There was a brief section on the pooping on the carpet exploits of Andrea's dog, Fetch. There was a brief section on the future career plans of Andrea, which included going to chef school and hopefully becoming the head chef of a major hotel or restaurant. Andrea's life was certainly an interesting one, especially following her divorce.

August also took this opportunity to think about a few things. He wanted to know what his favorite color was and a kitchen is a wonderful place to look for your favorite color. Every color imaginable exists within a kitchen. Beautiful orange bell peppers, the rich red of tomatoes and the sultry burgundy of cherries, the beautiful green of romaine lettuce, the beautiful blue of, well, to be honest, blue is not a color found very much in the kitchen. So, August took stock and decided on a color.

"My favorite color is ORANGE!!!"

This statement, the simplicity, solidarity and volume of it, stopped the girls in mid pillow talk. It startled them.

"Come again?" responded Monica, unsure if she had heard her boyfriend correctly.

"I've been going over the various colors in this room and thus far my choice for favorite color is orange. Specifically, I like the orange of the bell peppers in the fridge. I think orange is a beautiful color and it is thus far my favorite."

"Well I think orange is an excellent choice. It is extremely bright and cheerful and it is a wonderful choice for your favorite color," announced Andrea.

Monica was so excited that August had chosen anything, that she threw herself into his arms and kissed him full on the lips. August was both excited that he was getting open mouth kissed, and excited that he now had a favorite color and finally excited that that color was orange.

The two somewhat unstable individuals made their way back to the common room where Monica suggested that they watch a movie.

"Why don't we watch Toy Story?" replied August. For the second time that day, August was inundated with kisses for making the smallest of decisions.

So the two watched Toy Story, officially now for the fourth time, and once more August wandered around for the rest of the day exclaiming various lines from the film. It was annoying. It was obnoxious. Monica allowed it to continue although thoughts of bright flashing lights and candy jumped through her head, offering to put an end to the ramblings of her forgetful boyfriend. It was not that Monica did not care for him. The issue was that Monica had a very short temper, which kind of sucks when you have an amnesiac boyfriend.

It did not take long for August to stop thinking about his favorite color or the funny things that Tim Allen and Tom Hanks said in the film he had just watched, because a name popped into his head. The name was Ellen. He came to this brilliant conclusion while urinating. Dick in hand, August suddenly thought about Ellen. He didn't remember anything about Ellen. He didn't remember what she looked like. He didn't remember her relationship to him. He didn't remember what she did for a living and he didn't remember where she lived, but he remembered the name. So, he thought it was a good idea to ask his girlfriend if she knew anyone by the name of Ellen.

"Ellen?" she asked.

"Yes, Ellen."

Monica thought about it for a minute. She did know someone named Ellen. Her best friend was named Ellen, but surely this could not be the same Ellen that she knew. How would the two possibly know each other?

"I don't know anyone named Ellen actually. But we could always try to look for her."

"I don't even know if I really know someone named Ellen. I might just be imagining it. Or I might just have heard the name, and am trying to connect it to someone."

"Well, do you remember anything about her at all?"

"No. I don't remember if she is a blond or a brunette. I don't remember if she is my aunt or my girlfriend." August noticed the slight twinge in her face when he said that Ellen might be his girlfriend. "I really don't remember anything about her, but I do remember that name."

'It is not possible. It's not possible that this man could know my Ellen. It's not possible that MY man could know MY Ellen.'

August thought about this mystery woman. He thought about his very non-mystery woman, whom he liked very much. He thought about how she looked when he suggested that this Ellen might be his girlfriend. And then he thought about how she looked at him the rest of the time.

"I can only assume that I have an aunt Ellen." And with that August walked across the room, held his girlfriends face in his hands and kissed her. "If she is anything else, she's out of luck. Because I already have a girlfriend."

And with this wonderful line, this magnificent one-liner, August received an experience that, as far as he knew, he had never received before. He had in fact received this particular gift, from this particular woman, on more than one occasion. But as far as he knew, this was his first, and it was definitely his best. Amazingly enough, Monica had done this before as well, but not that she knew of. So she tried her best, and succeeded.

The next conundrum for August was music. He knew what music was. He knew music. But he didn't know about different sounds, different musicians. He could not have told you what jazz really was, although I don't think that anyone in this room could really tell you what jazz really was. He didn't know the Star Spangled Banner as sung by Brooke Hogan or Roseanne Barr and he did not know it as played by Jimi Hendrix, one of which, having not known, was a damned shame. As he sat beside Monica, herself humming *Afternoon Delight,* he began to think and began to question what music he might like.

"Monica, who is your favorite musician?"

Monica thought about it for a few moments. There were so many to choose from. It so depended upon the mood that struck her. There were many times when her answer would be Neil Young. Sunday afternoons, sitting on her couch drinking herbal tea, her favorite musician was Neil Young. But there were other times when her favorite musician was Paula Abdul. That's right, Paula Abdul. Paula Abdul was a wonderful musician to listen to on a Friday night, in your room, dancing around while your hair was drying. And then there were times… never mind.

"I don't know. There are so many great musicians. It would be difficult to choose just one. Do you have a favorite musician?"

"That's just the thing. I don't know. I was hoping you would help me choose."

And with that, August and Monica set about the task of trying to find his favorite musician. They decided that a chronological study of the subject would best suit them, that way they could ensure that they didn't miss anything. On this particular day, they were working their way through classical. Upon hearing of Dr. Wilkes 'unique' patient, the surgeons donated some of their operating room CD's to the cause. Beethoven, Brahms and Bach echoed through the hallways of their floor, while August made physical notes about the music, his likes and dislikes, and Monica made mental notes about the way August's hair fell across his brow and the way that he breathed when he was thinking. August's notes were about the fact that he liked classical music, but not enough to listen to it regularly. He would like to listen to it if he needed to rest, or if he were reading a book, or if he were in a bathtub, resting. But it was not something he would listen to outside of these parameters.

Sleep came quickly to August that evening. A little quicker than he would have liked, because it came from a lowering of his blood sugar level. In this daze, this moment between consciousness and unconsciousness, August saw clearly the color of Ellen's hair, her delicate face, and her beautiful lips. He saw these things and realized that Ellen Duncan had to be Monica Anderson's identical twin. She had to be. They were the spitting image of one another, except that Monica tended to wear her hair up. It was the only possible explanation.

Meanwhile, Monica was thinking eerily similar thoughts. 'How did August Feducialiter know Ellen Duncan? Was it possible that Ellen was having an affair on Dilbert with this man? Was it possible that August knew Dilbert? Was it possible that August knew where Dilbert was? Was it possible that Dilbert knew about August and left? OH MY GOD! That's it. Dilbert isn't lost, or missing. He left. Ellen was having an affair with August, Dilbert found out, struck him in the head, destroying his memory, and then fled, fearing prosecution. It was all coming into focus now. August was a victim, assuming he knew nothing about Dilbert. But he did not seem to her to be the type of man who would try to take another man's woman. August was most definitely a victim.' Monica decided that she would get to the bottom of this. She was a virtual Nancy Drew. She would get to the bottom of this.

August felt a little like he was on Law and Order. He felt a little like Roger Clemens sitting in front of a congressional hearing on HGH. He felt a little like he was being interrogated.

"You are certain you have never heard of anyone by the name of Dilbert Douglas?" asked Nancy Drew, as played by Monica Anderson.

"I am certain that I have never heard of anyone by the name of Dilbert Douglas. I have recently, according to my journal, read something by Dilbert Melville called *Moby Dick*, but that would be the extent of my Dilbertizing, my Dilbertology if you will."

"Interesting."

"What is so interesting about that?"

"Oh nothing. It's just that I have a friend named Dilbert, who I now realize described you exactly when referring to a dear friend of his."

"You think you might know one of my friends?" The thought excited August but also frightened him. The thought of not knowing someone who knew him was, for some unknown reason, extremely frightening to August.

"Well, maybe. But he has been missing for some time. In fact, it was my best friend that set me about looking for him."

"And what was her name? Maybe I know her."

And here it came to a precious boil. Monica had a couple of options. She could tell him that her best friend in the entire world was named Ellen Duncan and was likely the individual who may have been having an affair with August prior to his amnesia.

"Shmellen Dankin."

August began laughing. He laughed and laughed.

"Your best friends' name is Shmellen Dankin?"

"Yes. My best friends' name is Shmellen Dankin. Why is that so funny? Your name is August Feducialiter. Why is her name funny?"

"Yeah, but my name is made up. I made my name up. My name is born out of a series of mishaps and diseases. Her name is born out of birth. That's just stupid."

Monica was worried that August might see through her bluff. However, he didn't. He was clueless. He was an idiot. And it made Monica feel a little funny. It made her feel as though she was dating an absolute idiot. But he was devilishly handsome and was a great kisser, so she decided to stick it out. August also decided to stick it out, but for very different reasons. August was unaware that any of this was going on inside his girlfriend's seemingly innocent mind.

Dr. Wilkes met with August to really get into the issues surrounding his amnesia. Amnesia can typically be caused by three things; head trauma, ingestion of poison and emotional trauma. Dr. Wilkes had done a full toxicology screen when August was admitted. Unless the poison was ingested some time ago, it was not ingestion of poison. They had done multiple CAT scans when August was admitted. Unless the trauma was done some time ago, it was not head trauma. Therefore, it was only possible, unless the amnesia occurred some time ago, that emotional trauma was the cause of August's forgetting of the world. And as such, Dr. Wilkes met with August to discuss this possibility.

"August, do you have friends?"

"Yes. I have Andrea, and Jake, and Monica and you."

"That's nice, but do you know of any friends outside of the hospital you have. Siblings, or cousins, or friends. Anyone you can remember at all."

"Well there is no one that I can remember, but Monica thinks that one of her friends, a girl named Shmellen Dankin, might have a boyfriend named Dilbert who might know me. So, it is entirely possible that I do actually have a friend outside of this hospital."

Dr. Wilkes' heart leapt. Was the key to August Feducialiter really in this very hospital.

"What did she say about this Dilbert? Why does she think that you two might know each other?"

"She said that he had often described a man who fits my description."

Dr. Wilkes' heart sunk.

"Do you think it is possible that she was merely describing a similar individual? I mean, not to be rude August, but while you are indeed handsome, nothing about you is absolutely you. You have no defining characteristic that I would be able to use to describe you physically. What makes you think that it is anything more than a case of mistaken identity?"

August had considered the possibility that his current situation was nothing more than a matter of mistaken identity. But then, he felt it better to at the very least play out this farce.

"Dr. Wilkes, it is entirely possible that I am not the person that this man, Dilbert, spoke of. It is possible that they do not know me. It is possible that I am not this man. It is possible that no one in the entire world knows me. But it is the possibility that there is someone out there who knows me that keeps me going. It is the reason I am here in this office right now. So yes. I might be a similar individual. This may be a case of mistaken identity. But then what?"

August's statements were interesting. It made sense. Why not strive for everything you could possibly achieve? Why not live life thinking the best? Dr. Wilkes was a doctor and so his life was spent telling people that he was sorry. His life was spent telling people that he did everything that he could. His life was spent telling people that there was nothing more that could be done. But there were also many times where Dr. Wilkes was able to tell people some good news. He was able to tell people that all was not lost. He was able to tell people that it was a miracle that they were alive. He was able to tell people that they would have a full recovery despite any doubts that might exist about it. And so he thought, why not? Maybe this is the absolute best way to proceed. Maybe hope was more important than chances. Maybe it was more important to take a chance on life than it was to know the full extent of truth.

"Perhaps you are right August. Perhaps you are right. Perhaps the best course of action is to live life as though everything is going to be alright."

It was amusing to August that Dr. Wilkes used this particular phrasing. Monica and August were now making their way through the 1970's, musically that is, and one of the songs that August had fallen in love with was *Three Little Birds* from Exodus by Bob Marley. Marley was in August's 'Top 5' so far and the lessons that he taught through his music seemed universal, especially at this point.

"You're right Dr. Wilkes. Everything is going to be alright. Don't worry about a thing."

The session ended for the day, both men filled with a sense of hope for the future. August thought that perhaps he might be fine whether or not he was found. He might be okay even if he was not this friend that Monica spoke of. Meanwhile, Dr. Wilkes thought that August would certainly be alright. He did believe that August would be found. He felt assured of it. He knew it. He did not know how, but he knew that August was going to be alright.

Jake DiRossi was also thinking that August was going to be alright. However, he believed that he was going to be alright partially due to the influence of one Dr. Jake DiRossi. And what did Jake think was important to help August make it in the world? Slippers.

You might think that slippers are not important. You might think that slippers are of little importance. You might think that slippers are silly. But if you think any of these things you have never lived in a drafty apartment with hardwood and ceramics. Jake DiRossi had lived in a drafty apartment with hardwood and ceramics. And now he worked in a very cool hospital with all ceramic tile flooring. So he thought that August needed a good solid pair of slippers. Sure, he had a pair of slippers already, but they were those ridiculous little slip-on things that go over shoes, usually in the operating room.

"August, would you like to go shopping?"

"Where did you want to go shopping? I don't really have any money."

"I know that you don't have any money August. You are an amnesiac. You do not have anything. You don't even really have a name. I clearly do not expect you to pay for anything. I was thinking we could go slipper shopping."

"Slipper shopping?"

"Yeah, you know. Slippers. I think you need a good solid pair of slippers. We can look at other stuff too, but the floor is so cold here and since you might be in here awhile, I wanted you to have a nice pair of slippers."

"Sure. I just want to have a little rest. Do you want to come get me in about an hour?"

"Sounds good."

August went off to his room but it was not to have a rest. It was in fact to almost cry. You see, August now thought about the idea that he might be in this hospital for awhile. Suddenly, August became very aware of the fact that he did not have any specific hope for the future. Sure, everything was going to be alright...eventually...probably. But in the meantime, everything sort of sucked a little. He did have a girlfriend, but he didn't actually know her. He sort of knew her, but mostly just through what she told him and possibly what he wrote down, which she could have possibly told him to write down. In fact, there was very little about his life that August felt he had control of. But when it came down to it, what choice did he have. He had virtually no way of knowing who was on his side and out of all this sprang an unnatural sense of fear and foreboding. Paranoia set in and August began to wonder why Jake DiRossi was in fact taking him to buy slippers. It was not possible that Jake just wanted him to have warm, comfortable feet, although it was actually true that Jake just wanted him to have warm, comfortable feet. But August began to think that he needed to get away. He began thinking that he needed to make his escape into the wild.

If anyone had actually been watching the security cameras at the hospital, they would have seen a man walking through the halls with a slightly confused look on his face. He also had a slightly enthusiastic, focused look on his face. It was the look of a man who was going somewhere. When you combine a slightly confused look with a slightly enthusiastic, focused look you actually get a slightly ridiculous look that kind of looks like you are having a seizure. Unfortunately for August, people in the hospital knew who he was and knew that one of the issues that he had was a history of seizures. So, August was quickly returned to his room, where he got extremely tired, had a quick nap, and upon returning to consciousness, had no sweet clue that he was attempting to escape. Instead, Dr. Jake DiRossi entered August's room and told him that he wanted to take him out shopping, possibly for slippers, and possibly for anything else that he might like. August thought it was a great idea and went to the mall with him.

On the way to the mall, Jake DiRossi got to know August, as much as was possible given the fact that August was trying very hard to get to know himself. So they chatted. August learned all about Jake's life, his sad romantic woes, his current romantic exploits and his wishes for his romantic future. He learned that Jake was a collector. Jake collected hats and had a current collection of over 350. Most were baseball caps, but there were also a number of different ones including several top hats and an interesting collection of beanies. Jake learned virtually nothing about August. He asked August if he remembered liking any sports.

"Like what?" asked the very poor trivia partner?

"You know... baseball, basketball, football, hockey. I'm a baseball man myself. I played college ball during my undergrad. Third base."

"I don't really know. I do remember what each of those sports are. And I have a vague memory of each of them. But I don't know which I prefer. I have a feeling that I was a hockey fan. I couldn't tell you why. I mean. I don't really remember ever having seen a game. I don't remember ever having played a game, but I can see the ice, and the players."

"Isn't that weird? Not really remembering anything like that."

"Well, obviously it's weird. I mean, you can remember certain games you played in and you can remember most things about your life. Me, I can't remember what I ate yesterday, what my favorite color is or my own fucking name."

"I'm sorry August. I didn't mean to upset you. I guess I just can't imagine what you are dealing with right now. I'm sorry, we can talk about something else."

"It's fine Jake. I don't mind talking about it. And I'm not really getting upset. It's just that sometimes fuck gets the point across like no other word quite can."

"I would tend to agree August. The word certainly gets its point across. Anyways, lets talk about hockey. I love hockey. Not quite as much as I love baseball. But I still really like it."

"I think hockey is my favorite, but I am not really sure. I mean, like I say, I can't really remember anything about hockey. I just have this vague concept of liking to watch people skate around on the white ice. I like the sound. There is something very soothing about the sound. Every time they make a cut, you can hear that sweet sound."

"Do you think you'd like to go to a game sometime?"

"What do you mean? Like a real, actual hockey game?"

"Yes August, like a real, actual hockey game. My old man has season tickets to the Bruins, I'm sure that I could get us a couple of tickets for a game sometime once the season starts."

"Are you for real? You would actually take me to a game?"

"Absolutely August. That's what friends are for."

Now August had friends. He had Monica. But he always had the feeling that Monica was hiding something from him. And he had Andrea. But he only really got to see Andrea when he was hungry. And he had Jake. Jake was the first friend that August had that he felt had no selfish reasons for being his friend. August felt as though he could confide in Jake. Mind you, he had nothing to really confide. August's life was very much without secrets. Most of August's secrets were as much secrets from himself as they were secrets from everyone else. In fact, most of the secrets that surrounded August's life were secrets not kept by him but kept from him. However, he felt as though if there were a secret that had to be kept, and a friend that needed to be confided in, that friend would be Dr. Jake DiRossi.

Jake in the meantime felt very sad for August. He seemed like a really decent guy. He seemed like someone that Jake could definitely be friends with. And Jake did not have a large number of friends. Sure, he was handsome. Sure he was polite. Sure he was rich. But for several years he had whittled away any friends that he had by letting his girlfriend, the same girlfriend who would eventually cheat on him, control his life. As such, Jake DiRossi was in need of a friend. And August Feducialiter was in need of a friend. And so it was that the two became friends.

The trip to the mall was very interesting. Firstly, August had never been to a mall before, as far as he knew. He was relatively unfamiliar with the mall, both in terms of its layout as well as the expected flow of events. For example, when two individuals walk towards each other in a mall, each individual should follow the acceptable traffic flow by keeping to their right. I have often wondered what happens in Britain, but that is not really the issue here. So, August kept bumping into people until Jake explained to him the whole 'keep to your right' thing. Once this was explained to him, August's mall experience was far more enjoyable, both for himself, and for others. There were other subtleties to mall shopping that August did not seem to really be picking up exactly. Jake, for example, had a rough idea of what stores he wanted to go into, what stores he might want to go into and what stores he did not at all want to go to. However, August had no idea what stores were suitable, interesting, affordable or ridiculous. So when

Jake told August that they could go into any store that August wanted and that, as long as the prices were not alarming, Jake would be willing to buy some things for him, this was entirely useless because setting August loose in a mall and telling him that they could go into any store they wanted was like asking someone who didn't speak English to give you a review of the film that they just watched in English, IN ENGLISH. And this is how it came to be that August and Jake found that a proposed two-hour trip to the mall turned into a relatively unplanned six-hour trip to the mall.

They walked through every store. They walked through greeting card stores, through women's lingerie shops, bookstores and jewelry stores, through sporting good stores, clothing stores and toy stores. Jake spent his first hour excited. August seemed to be legitimately enjoying himself and given the few purchases that Jake had made thus far, it seemed like a sound investment in happiness. Following this there was an hour of mild enjoyment where August seemed to at least be enjoying himself and Jake spent nothing. Then there was a half hour session where August attempted to decide what food court delicacy he would like to sample. And it is here that I definitely understand August's pain. On more than one occasion I have wandered back and forth in front of the food court restaurants, attempting to make the decision between barely warm French fries, cardboard flavored pizza, a couple of pieces of fake meat masquerading as hamburgers and several pieces of barely green lettuce pretending to be a salad. August finally settled on cardboard pizza.

Following the brief foray into mall dining, August resumed his shopping. Jake began to hate August. He did not necessarily hate August. In fact, he really liked August. He absolutely loved August and he believed that in the long run, the two could possibly become great friends. But at this moment, he hated August. He found himself picturing various ways that August could possibly die in the mall. One thought was that the person grinding keys could suddenly let go of the key they were working on which would then become a shining projectile shooting through the air and lodging itself in August's windpipe. He then thought that there was an off chance of an escalator malfunction that could leave August without any limbs. Jake would still be friends with August if he had no arms or legs. In many ways, they might even be better friends than they are now. If anything, it would be easier for them to hang out. An individual with no arms and no legs is much easier to hang out with then someone without. For example, if you are hanging out with someone with no arms and no legs and they get really drunk, they are less likely to fall down because they are more or less, down. Also, if they do fall down, they are very easy to get back up. And if you then had to put said armless, legless friend in a cab, I can only assume that it would be far easier to put them in said cab. Sure, it might not be great for August. But then again, he could probably just start over again with a new identity. He'd done it before. He could likely do it again.

Following this, there were several hours of minor success. August found a shirt that he really liked that said, "My other shirt is a tux." It was cheesy and it was silly, but August figured that he could forget anything that anyone said or felt about his outfit. It was the best part of August's amnesia. To be fair, it was really the only good part, so when I say it was the best part, I am really only stating that it was the one part about being an amnesiac that didn't suck. It is absolutely true that August's life sucked, but the strangest part was that he was blissfully unaware that there was anything really wrong with his life. And thus, August decided, mid-mall, to don his new "My other shirt is a tux" shirt.

Jake DiRossi was now walking down the mallway with a young man who appeared to be mentally deficient and had absolutely no fashion sense. So, it made Jake DiRossi even more attractive than his 250 sit-ups a day and his hour of cardio ever could. It makes him look like a member of Big Brother's, Big Sister's and nothing attracts the ladies like a man who is willing to give back. As they entered Bed, Bath and Beyond to search for a pair of slippers, which had been the primary purpose of said trip to the mall in the first place, Jake's ability to attract beautiful young women seemed to be further enhanced, as evidenced by the smashing young lady working the footwear department. He determined that she was hitting on him by the fact that she paid virtually no attention to the three customers currently wandering the store and looking for shoes. Instead, she came over to Jake and his obviously mentally deficient younger brother and asked if they needed help.

"Well, we're looking for a pair of slippers for my friend here."

"And are we looking for comfort or warmth?"

This seems like a question that would best be asked of the individual who actually wanted slippers. However, it was clearly not asked of August. It was asked of the very patient doctor who was traveling with him.

"Well, I think we're looking for a combination of comfort, warmth and style. I mean, he wants to look cool, but he needs warmth and he wants something that is comfortable to move around in. He's a patient at the hospital so he wants something that is good for the floor there."

"Oh, I see. Is he your brother or something?"

"Oh no. I'm a doctor at the hospital."

"I see. Well, let's see what we can help you with… I'm sorry, I didn't catch your name."

"It's Jake. Jake DiRossi."

"Nice to meet you Jake. I'm Elizabeth."

"It's a pleasure to meet you Elizabeth."

The two young beautiful people stared into each other's eyes. With all this staring into each other's eyes they missed the fact that August had wandered off. It began with a brief foray into footwear, followed by a trip through sheets. Following this, August began to work his way into towels. Then, August went beyond Bed, Bath and Beyond. Meanwhile inside the store, Jake and Elizabeth were getting to know each other. Jake learned that she was a student at Boston College majoring in Political Science. He also determined that she was not the sharpest tool in the shed and he doubted that there was much chance of her becoming the nation's first female President. But she was very good looking and was wearing a nice low cut shirt so he paid careful attention to everything that she said, more or less. He paid very careful attention once she asked where his patient had gone.

August wandered from store to store but felt somewhat ill. He realized that this was likely due to the cardboard pizza he had settled on in the end. So he decided that a trip to the trip to the mall in this case included a very important trip to the washroom. He made his way through a hallway that seemed very familiar to him. (He would never really discover that it looked familiar because it was identical to the mall hallway scene in Terminator 2, which he would eventually learn was his third favorite movie. We'll talk about the first two later). At the end of the hallway he found the derelict and oft-ignored washroom. He settled in for the long haul.

    Jake began to work his way through the mall; backtracking through stores that August had shown some interest in. He went into each and every store that they had gone in, asking if anyone had seen his friend, the slightly slow seeming young man who he had been traveling through the mall with. Few remembered Jake, none remembered August. Jake began to worry. First, he worried about what could have happened to August. There was a certain part of Jake that worried very much for August's safety. As has previously been established, the two had become good friends and Jake was worried that August might be hurt. Then he thought of the whole ordeal from another perspective. I mean, sure, August and Jake were friends. But also, Jake was a doctor. He liked being a doctor. When it came down to it. Jake could virtually buy new friends, but he was also responsible for August's well being while they were outside the hospital. As such, if August went missing, or worse, if he died, Jake would be blamed and would likely lose his license. So, his search for August became less of a search for his friend and more a search for his career, which was quickly slipping from his grasp. Have you ever lost your keys? Really frustrating isn't it? Well, now imagine that instead of losing your keys, you lost a person. Now imagine that you were professionally responsible for said person and that that person was also dangerously ill. Jake DiRossi felt absolutely sick.

    And then, between the food court and the dry cleaning shop, Jake saw him. Wandering around like some sort of escaped mental patient, which I guess he was, Jake approached August.

    "Oh my god August, you had me so worried."

"I'm sorry, do I know you?"

"Fantastic. You've lost your memory again. Ok, my name is Jake DiRossi and I am one of your doctors."

"If I'm a medical patient, why am I at the mall?"

"We came to the mall to look for a pair of slippers for you and you wandered off while we were in Bed, Bath and Beyond."

"Hmmm. Sounds possible but how do I know this for sure?"

"Well, since you have no memory whatsoever, there is no real way to know for sure. You just have to trust me."

August decided that since he did in fact have no memory whatsoever and he could not really come up with any reason why this man would be attempting to steal him and since that man seemed to know that he in fact did not have any memory, he would go with this man. So it was that August returned to the hospital with Jake DiRossi, a bad case of indigestion from food court pizza and no slippers, which had been the primary reason for the trip to the mall in the first place.

Monica was happy to see August upon his return. Every second that August spent away from Monica was another second that he might remember who he was. He had already said her name.

She embraced August with verve when he entered her room. Based upon his confusion, she assumed he had had a loss (what Monica called it when August forgot everything that he had learned thus far).

"You don't know me do you?"

August began to laugh, a deep hearty laugh that started just above his groin, resonated up through his stomach and came shooting out of his jaw. It was at this point that Monica realized that August knew exactly who she was.

"You asshole" said Monica, punching him gingerly on the arm. "That's mean."

"Well, I figure it's important, in my position, to have a decent sense of humor."

Monica figured this was probably true so she switched her tactics from gingerly punches to the arm to aggressive kisses to the mouth. He really was an excellent kisser, thought Monica. He was very warm and he didn't do what most guys did with their tongue. Most guys use the exact same tactic, over and over again. For some, it's the swirl. The swirl is an okay move, if you use it a little. But some guys use the tongue swirl and the tongue swirl only. And some of those guys only ever go in one direction. So, it's kind of like making out with a blender. And I don't know if any of you have ever made out with a blender, but I would not recommend it. Then there are the silent tongue assassins. These are the guys who will be making out with you, using only their lips and then, when you least expect it, they suddenly thrust their tongue into their mouth. It is kind of like a dog that suddenly bites you after you have been petting it for a generous amount of time. The dog might not bite hard, it might even kind of tickle. But it will also scare the shit out of you and it is unlikely that you will want to continue petting the dog and you will likely kick the dog outside and not let it sleep in your bed anymore, because no one wants to get the shit scared out of them. Finally, and these are probably the worst, are the tongue wrestlers. These geniuses think that the best thing to do is to try to fight off your tongue while you are trying to play with theirs. They are the perfect combatants. If you go to your left, they cut you off. If you go to your right, they cut you off. And eventually, you just don't want to wrestle anymore and you tell them to go away and that they are pricks.

What made August such a great kisser was that he did none of these things. Instead of a silent assassin, tongue wrestler or mouth blender, he was a lover. He caressed her tongue with his, asking her to kiss him back and then accepting her answer, whatever it might be. It was beautiful really. And this was one of the many reasons that Monica loved August enough to not tell him who he really was.

We cut away now to talk about the rest of the Douglas clan, namely Dilbert Douglas' mother and father, Nathaniel and Elizabeth Douglas.

The two had come to a variety of conclusions during this particular French vacation. Firstly, they clearly did not love each other. It would seem that their marriage was a sham and that they were whittling their days away in a loveless relationship. Secondly, they loved alcohol. Without alcohol, they likely would not have made it this far into their marriage. Without alcohol, they probably would be much more upset that they did not love, nay, almost hated each other. Thirdly, they realized that they needed to end their marriage so that they could attempt to live happy lives. Fourthly, they realized that they missed their son dearly, the one thing that they both had in common, aside from the revelations already discussed. And they decided that they would call him. When there was no answer, they were not immediately concerned. They assumed he was out and they went about their aforementioned pattern of alcoholism and adultery, albeit understood, expected, mutual and excused adultery. Obviously both sides would probably use it as an excuse during their divorce, but for now, it was very much excused.

At almost the exact same time, Craig and Delores Duncan were thinking of their lovely daughter Ellen. They were thinking that they had not been back to Boston in a very long time. They were thinking that it might be time to return to Boston for a little visit. To be honest, Craig Duncan was more interested in traveling to the east coast of Canada for go karting than he was interested in traveling to the east coast of the United States for a visit with his daughter. It is of course not the case that Craig Duncan did not love his daughter but rather he simply thought that she could wait. However, Delores Duncan did not believe she could wait, and thus decided on a trip to Boston. She called her lovely, beautiful, vivacious and sometimes interesting daughter to inform her of their somewhat sudden, somewhat surprising trip to Boston. When her daughter didn't answer, she just assumed that she was working. She left a message, asking Ellen to call when she got in.

"Hey sweetie. It's your mother, remember me (subtle dig at the fact that her daughter rarely calls)? I just wanted to say that your father thought it would be a good idea to take a trip up to Boston to see you. Just wondering what your work schedule was like and when you might be free. Anyways, give me a call. We never hear from you anymore (slight change in voice to reflect the almost tears from her mother)."

Unfortunately for Delores, Ellen was not at work. Ellen was actually sitting in the entertainment room of a hospital teaching Canasta to someone whom she had recently met and had been dating for over six years. It was a conundrum and one that would not be easily resolved.

"I don't really think this is your game," offered up Ellen, or Monica, or whatever you want to call her.

Given the results of their Canasta playing thus far, this would seem to be one of the more obvious statements that Monica had made as of late. However, August took it for an insightful observation and responded thus.

"It would appear that you are right. I don't think that I am very good at Canasta. Maybe I'm not good at cards, or maybe I'm not good at games in general. There are any number of possibilities to why I am not good at Canasta. To be totally honest, it could be that you are in some way cheating me."

"Cheating you? How could I be cheating you?"

"Well, you just taught me the game. You could be changing the rules as we go just to suit your needs. I'm not saying you are cheating me. I'm just saying that you could be cheating me. Obviously I don't think that you would be so cruel as to cheat me out of winning the game you just taught me, given my circumstances."

However, for the first several rounds, that is exactly what had happened. Monica did not like to lose and figured that this was a great opportunity to finally be a winner. Monica had never really been a winner. Ellen was great at every game they had ever played together and to be honest, that got pretty annoying, pretty fast. This relationship was far more rewarding than the one that she had carried on with Ellen. It was interesting to imagine that the pretend person's relationship with the amnesiac who did not know who he was, was more rewarding than the pretend person's relationship with her other personality and in fact, probably more rewarding and loving that the relationship that had previously existed between the two real individuals who were currently involved in the semi-pretend relationship with their semi-pretend personalities. I do not pretend that this is not the most confusing situation of all time, but what are ya gonna do?

Dr. Wilkes ate his breakfast early on Tuesday. He got up at 6:48am, which was about forty-two minutes earlier than he would typically wake up on a Tuesday morning. He ate two eggs, 3 slices of bacon, a small dollop of beans and two pieces of whole-wheat toast with crunchy peanut butter. This was Dr. Wilkes favorite breakfast outside of French toast and French toast was a far more difficult breakfast to make and to be honest, the additional forty two minutes that Dr. Wilkes had procured for himself with his early rise, would not have allowed Dr. Wilkes, an absolutely awful cook, to create anything that remotely resembled French toast. So, following his delicious breakfast, Dr. Wilkes made his way to the hospital. He made his way to the hospital with the express purpose of discovering August's secret identity. He had a hint. Monica knew something, And he would discover what the thing was.

"Monica. August had suggested to me that you might know something about his past? He told me this, but I think he has since forgotten it, and I wanted to talk to you about this."

Monica became very nervous. Her hands began to sweat. She felt cold, and then warm, and then cold again, and then finally warm once more. She immediately become frightened and afraid. And then she felt guilty. She felt guilty because she had lied to her boyfriend. She had lied to the doctors. She had lied to everyone. She had betrayed her best friend.

"What do you mean?"

"I think you know what I mean Monica. You told August that you had a friend and that that friend might know him. Do you remember that?"

"Oh THAT. That's not exactly what I told him. I told him that I had a friend who had a boyfriend who REMINDED me of him. It wasn't that I knew him. He just got a little confused. He gets confused a lot."

Dr. Wilkes did not in any way believe that Monica was telling the truth. He had become suddenly and inexplicably suspicious of her. He did not know what it was. But there was something about her that just said, I am a filthy liar.

"I see. So it was all a misunderstanding?"

"Right."

Monica knew that Dr. Wilkes did not believe her. Dr. Wilkes knew that Monica was lying. No one knew what to do about either of these two facts. And so they went about their day.

August was sleeping. It was 3:30pm when he awoke. It is strange how being in a hospital will have a direct impact on your ability to maintain regular sleeping habits. I have been in hospital before and found that no matter what my normal sleeping habits were before entering that eggshell, crème and beige abyss, my sleeping habits would immediately change to "random naps mid-afternoon" and "occasional falling asleep mid-sentence." There was a lot of mid in a hospital. And I hated it. August had a much friendlier demeanor while he was in his hospital stay than I had when I was in mine. So, it was not odd that August was spending his afternoon set adrift on memory bliss. When he awoke, he found Dr. Wilkes sitting at the foot of his bed, reading through charts.

"Good morning doctor."

"Afternoon August. How are you feeling today?"

"Well, I'm not going to lie. I feel great."

At this point was the aforementioned, what the hell is going on scenario, where August learned that he was in a hospital and that he had no memory. They went over all the preliminaries. August did not feel particularly well. However, he did not feel bad, and he did not want to be a bother, so he simply said that he was great. It wasn't a lie per se, but at the same time it was not 100% truth.

"That's excellent. I wanted to work with you today to try to get some of those memories flowing, seeing what we could do to figure out who August Feducialiter is."

"That sounds superb."

"First. Do you have any idea how old you are?"

"What?"

"Your age. Do you have any idea how old you might be?"

"Well, I don't think I'm particularly old. I don't know. How do you judge how old you are?"

This was a difficult question and one that August had not particularly considered. Can you feel your age? Is it something innate or do you just count the memories you have and subtract by one hundred. It was as unique a question as was the question of your favorite color but more difficult to ascertain the answer to. One was a qualitative question. A qualitative question can be changed. It's like figure skating. Figure skating can be judged and you can say, "I really thought that was a nice triple axle" or "their double sow cow (going to be honest and say I don't have a sweet clue how it is spelled)." But if they then said, how tall was the figure skater, you have to make a quantitative judgment. You need to figure out how tall they are by making a guess. You have something to go on, but it's still a guess. Then if you were asked how old she was, you would have to make a far less educated guess. Sure, you might know some things about her that might lead you to a better understanding of how old she is. But the combination of plastic surgery and makeup make knowing virtually impossible. So, August had to think. He knew that he had not had plastic surgery. Well, then he thought about it. Maybe he had had plastic surgery. Fuck. He would never really know. He started feeling around his face. He assumed that there would be some sort of scar, some sort of mark or indication that he had had surgery. But there was not so he figured that he had never gone "under the knife." He also discovered in his wanderings that he was not wearing makeup. Well, it was possible that he could be wearing makeup, but it didn't feel like it.

"I think I'm about twenty six."

"Twenty six eh? Why's that?"

"I don't know. I just think I feel twenty-six. I don't know how twenty five feels, and I don't know what twenty seven feels like, but I think twenty six feels pretty much like how I feel right now."

Dr. Wilkes marveled at the young, twenty-six? year old before him. He was, to say the least, unique. He was, to say the least, strange. He was, to say the least, the oddest patient that Dr. Wilkes had ever treated, for anything.

"Well, that is an interesting way to look at it."

"Is there another way I should look at it?"

"I don't know. I would think you would try to… Well, hell. I really don't know of any other way."

"Exactly. If there is some magic test that we can run that tell you how old I am, like cut me open and count my number of rings or something, please tell me now, and we'll figure this out. In the meantime, this is what I have. My feelings."

It was true. Feelings. Gut. These were the things that August had to go on. He could not recall his last birthday, or any birthday before for that matter. He didn't remember prom, or graduation, or summer vacations, or his high school sweetheart. He remembered waking up, he remembered the doctor telling him he could not remember anything, (thanks for the update doc) and that was it. Everything was a feeling. Dr. Wilkes asked a few more questions. August gave a few more perfunctory answers and then Dr. Wilkes told him about the diary, and then he left August to become reacquainted with his life.

He read over the diary and tried to become familiar with his history and his life. He became familiar with his new girlfriend and his other friends within the hospital. In the end, he felt confused. He was wondering what the hell he was supposed to do about all of this. He was wondering where he was supposed to go from here. His wonderings were creating little in the way of answers so he decided to switch from wonderings to wanderings. He got out of bed, put on a pair of slippers that he found beside his bed, and left his new home. He walked down the hall, through the hall that had become his home. The walls were painted a dull purple. The type of purple where you have to ask questions like, "who the hell invented this shade of purple?" It wasn't grape. It was bright. It wasn't friendly or warm. It was not Barney. It was the color that Barney would throw up. If Barney had a few two many, Barney would throw up the pale purple that covered these walls. The interesting thing about hospitals is that they color code everything so that you know where you are. Once August left the "barney throw up area," he entered "banana peach zone" where bananas and peaches mated on the walls. Whatever happened to blue, green and red? Like, seriously. What the hell happened to primary colors? Why is mango a color? Mango is not a color. Mango is a delicious Caribbean fruit. Mango is an aromatic flavor of chutney. Mango is not a color that should grace the walls of a hospital. And yet it does. August made his way through each zone and made his way to the cafeteria. When he arrived there, he was greeted by Andrea, his cafetorium friend.

"Hi August."

"Hello Andrea." He had learned her name from the diary of his life.

"And what is on the menu for today?"

"Isn't that really a question I should be asking you as the purveyor of fine foods?"

"Well, from a food preparation standpoint, yes. But I more so meant from a general life perspective. As in, what are your general plans for today? A sort of, what is the menu for your life?"

"Ahh, THAT menu. Well, I'll tell you what… nothing really. I have no particular plans. To be honest, I'm a wanderer, yeah, a wanderer. I roam around and round and round and round and round and round."

"That's a great song."

"What?"

"That song. It's a favorite of mine."

"I don't think I remember what song it is."

"It's a song from the sixties, by Dion."

August remembered that. It hit him like a mac truck. Everyone always says that. Everyone always says, "it hit them like a mac truck." What a ridiculous concept. How does something hit someone like a mac truck? A mac truck would cause a tremendous amount of damage and when a revelation hits you, it's not like it does a tremendous amount of damage. It does not leave you splayed across the I-95 like a raccoon that did not quite make it. It is more like a memory. It's like suddenly remembering something. At worst, it's like a minor electric shock, the kind of shock you would get if someone walked across a carpet, rubbing their socked feet on the carpet and then touched you on the bare skin. You would kind of jump a little, and then you would be like… wow, that was weird, and then you would be fine again. Mac truck my ass.

"I know this song."

"I know. You were singing it."

"No, I mean I actually remember that song. I remember this actual song."

"Well, that's good."

"Good? Good? It's fantastic. This is the first time I have remembered something in a long time… as far as I remember. I remember making out with someone to that song."

"Do you remember who you were making out with? Because that would sort of be a break through."

August thought about it. He could almost see her. He could smell her. She smelt like peppermint. He could taste her. She tasted like juicy fruit. But he couldn't quite see her. He could see her hair. Her hair reminded him of someone else. It looked very seventies. It was almost feathered. It reminded him of someone. He looked over at Andrea. Andrea did not have feathered, dirty blonde hair, so it was not Andrea. It almost looked like Monica. Then out of nowhere, he saw her face. It was Monica. He had to see her, NOW.

It is important to clean up spills immediately. For example, of you spilled a small amount of milk on the floor, it would be necessary to clean that up as soon as possible. For example, if an amnesiac were to suddenly remember something from his past and then leapt up to run upstairs to find his girlfriend and ask why he remembered making out with her outside of the hospital, he could slip on that milk. And slip he did. One leg left the ground and made its way up into the air. Once it got there, it dragged the other leg with it and it left August upside down. Once upside down, August landed on the back of his head and suddenly became sleepy. Well, to be fair, he actually became asleep, but close enough. Andrea screamed and called for help. Help came and August was taken back to emergency.

When August awoke, he did not remember that he once made out with Monica outside the hospital. He did not remember any songs, let alone any songs by Dion to which he knew the words. He did have a headache. A really bad headache. A stupendously horrible headache. He had the worst headache he could ever remember. He had the only headache he could ever remember. And it sucked.

"What happened?" he asked of the first person he saw upon regaining consciousness, which happened to be Dr. Wilkes.

"You got a concussion. You slipped and fell in the cafeteria."

"I don't remember that at all."

It made Dr. Wilkes actually laugh, which did not sit very well with his patient.

"I'm sorry, is there something funny about the fact that I can't remember a fucking thing about my accident?"

"I'm sorry August. It's just that... well... you are here in this hospital being treated for amnesia. You never remember anything."

This did seem a little funny to August, but he still felt as though his position could have been handled with a little more delicacy. But that could be dealt with at a later date.

"So who am I doc?"

"Well, that's one of the problems. We don't really know who you are."

"But you know my name?"

"Not exactly. We gave you the first name August because you were brought in in August. So, we named you August. You decided on your last name, Feducialiter."

"Wait a minute. You don't even know who I really am?"

"That would be, unfortunately, correct."

"Well then. I don't really know what to say."

"August, don't worry about anything. We are taking very good care of you here."

"Then why does my head hurt?"

"Well, you tried to run out of the cafeteria. Not entirely sure why. And when you went to run you slipped and fell and bounced your head off the floor."

August suddenly felt as though the hospital might not be the safest place in the world for him. August suddenly felt like a hospital was a silent, but deadly, death trap. He felt like the hospital was the worst possible place for him to be and that he needed to escape. He felt as though he needed to burst out of the bed shouting 'Free Tibet' and run down the hall faster than a cheetah or any other swift moving cat, ripping apart every ounce of the hospital as he ran. He wanted to leave and he wanted to leave right now.

"What are you thinking August?"

"Oh... Nothing, just thinking. So, what do we do now? Do you guys have any leads on who I might be?"

"Not exactly."

Sometimes when someone says not exactly it means that they have a basic idea but they do not know exactly what is going on. This means that there is some slight deviation between reality and perceived reality. However, there are other times, this time being one of those other times, when not exactly actually means that there is no slight deviation between reality and perceived reality. It means that there is a Grand Canyon-esque deviation between the two. It means that the difference between reality and perceived reality is much like the difference between English and Swahili. They are both languages, essentially, but no one has any idea what the hell you are talking about. And when Dr. Wilkes said 'not exactly', this is the sort of 'not exactly' that Dr. Wilkes meant. The latter, rather than the former. August, not knowing the difference between the two, was still curious.

"So, what do you know about me?"

"Nothing."

Suddenly, August Feducialiter was far less confused. Everything seemed pretty clear, as much as absolute lack of clarity could be compared with clarity. For example, rather than saying that August understood, it would be fair to say that he now understood all the things that no one truly understood.

"You do have a diary."

At first, this information came as a mere annoyance to August. Whoop-di-fucking-do. I have a diary. I guess now I can tell it my innermost secrets (of which August had none), my dreams (of which August could not remember), and my secret desires (of which he could not recall). August failed to see the practical application of the diary at this point. He failed to recognize its potential. He failed to discover, on his own, the possibilities that this diary offered. However, as Dr. Wilkes explained a little bit of how August had used the diary thus far, August began to discover the importance of this volume on his life, certainly more interesting that his medical file.

And August read. He read about everything and everyone and assumed that at some point all this would become fact for him rather than fiction. He assumed that at some point he would think of this book as a collection of things that he already knew rather than a compendium of facts he neither knew nor understood. But August read. And he began to learn about himself, the other characters that filled his little world and most importantly to him, a girlfriend. It was an interesting story, filled with unique characters and poignant details about each. He began to understand more and more and began to believe less and less that he would ever understand what the hell was going on. And this made August fearful.

"Would you mind giving me a little time to digest all of this information?"

"Sure."

And with that, Dr. Wilkes got up and left the room, leaving August to his own devices. In this case, August was using the opportunity to plan his escape. He instantly knew that he could remain in this hospital no longer. He was clearly not being cured and he had suffered trauma to the head, heart and soul since arriving. It was clear that the open road was the place for him. Now, when I say 'it was clear', I mean that it seemed clear to August. Of course, it would be clear to any physician that the hospital was the best place for August, the best place for any individual who was an amnesiac and had suffered any sort of semi-serious head trauma. But August was not a physician. He was not a doctor in any sense, not even a social sciences doctor, which has never made any sense to me by the way. A doctor is someone who can assist you when you are feeling ill in some way. For example, a doctor of psychology or psychiatry might be able to help you when you are feeling mentally ill. A doctor of medicine could assist you with a cold, or the flu, or any other physical illness. But, what the fuck is a doctor of English going to cure you of? I suppose if you were suffering from writer's block, or poem….itis, then a doctor of English might be able to assist you, but that is ridiculous. Any doctor who can't make you feel mentally or physically healthier than you were to begin with is not doctor. I don't care that you had to spend three years in school doing a master's of English and then another five years doing your 'doctorate', you are not a doctor. Some of you might now be saying, Jim, if my name were Jim, you need to do a little more research because you can do a 'doctorate' in four years. Yes, you can. But nobody does asshole, so back off.

Anyways, it would be fairly obvious to anyone with their intellectual capacities intact that August should not leave the hospital, but August was more or less without his intellectual capacities. And as such, he left.

August's exodus from the hospital was easy. He got up, pulled on the pants that he found next to his bed, took off the ever-lovely Johnny shirt and replaced it with a shirt that he was sad to realize likely belonged to him. He stood up, pulled on the socks and shoes that were also located beside his bed and walked. He walked out into the hall where he found a sign that said 'EXIT'. He followed the directions typically provided for guests and instead used them as a means of escape. After multiple turns through what appeared to be the exact same halls, (all hospital hallways look identical), August saw the main entrance. He saw slips of sunlight sliding down through cracks in the clouds and finding their way onto the pavement. He was so very close. He was feet, inches, millimeters, seconds and nanoseconds from the space between the real world and this fake, antiseptic hospital. It was at this point that August heard his name. Well, what August and the person calling out his name knew to be his name.

"August!"

August spun on a dime, (no really, there happened to be a dime underneath his left shoe, which actually allowed for a smoother spin) and was face to face with a face that he did not recall. Apparently the look of confusion/surprise/disinterest was enough to let the caller of names know that she was not familiar to the callee.

"It's me, Monica. Your girlfriend. Where are you going?"

August did remember reading about her in the diary. And she was just as lovely in person as she was in his little book of life. But this was not the time for love affairs. He had to make his escape.

"There's no time for talking. Will you come with me?"

"Where?"

"It shouldn't matter where."

The decision was now on Monica. Would she stay here in the hospital or make a Bonnie and Clyde type break for it with her boyfriend. She decided on the latter, took his hand and ran out the front door with him.

This is the end of section one. Many of you were blissfully unaware that this book was split into any discernible sections, but I hope now you realize how important it is that you pay attention. If you have not paid attention to section one, you might as well put this book down now and reinvest your time in something more possible, because if you don't know who Jake is, don't know where the Douglas' are and don't know why Monica and Ellen have never met, you have now wasted your time and mine. Thank you.

Monica began to wonder what they should do. And moreover, where they should go. They could not go to her house. It was simply not possible. She could take him to Ellen's house to stay, but there was that underlying fear, jumping up into her subcocles that suggested that August might in fact be Dilbert Douglas, the very man that she had been sent out by her best friend, Ellen Duncan, to find. She felt horrible. It made her sick to her stomach. It made her feel awful. It made her feel like a disgusting individual. But, she also had a boyfriend now. Having a boyfriend was a big deal for her. She had never had a boyfriend before and she would not let anything, including her best friend get in her way. However, this still left a problem. Where would they go? How would they live? She had no idea what to do next. And she had one friend; one person who could possibly help her, and that was her best friend. It might require swallowing pride and friendship together but it was the only option. So she made her way to her best friends house. But she had a plan.

"Why do I have to wait outside? This is your friend right? So why would she mind if I came in?"

"I just have to clear things with her."

"How do you even know she is home?"

"I don't. But she left me a key."

"So she might not be home, but I'm still not allowed to come in?"

"That's right."

August could not help but think that this was ridiculous. He could not help but think that there was something wrong here. And yet, who was he to question the beautiful girl before him. So he gave her a kiss, promised to stay very still and very quiet, and she left him to go upstairs to her friend's home. August sat.

Monica entered her best friend's apartment and saw right away that bringing August upstairs would have been a huge mistake. Upon entering the home, she found a fairly large picture of August. Strangely enough, it was of her and August. She did not remember ever meeting him, but she must have. She found a number of pictures of her, of August, and of her and August strewn about the house, which she confiscated. She hid all the pictures and decided that she could now invite her boyfriend upstairs. She was somewhat worried that Ellen might return home. But it was a risk she had to take.

"So now I'm allowed to come upstairs?"

"Why are you being so difficult? Do you have a pressing engagement down here? Do you have an appointment I don't know about that you need to attend? Do you want to come upstairs or not?"

"Well of course I want to come upstairs. I just don't understand what's happening."

"You don't always have to understand what's going on around you."

This was good because August rarely understood what was going on around him. He had actually become relatively accustomed to this extremely and uniquely unique lifestyle. He had grown dependant on his diary to tell him who he could trust and who he couldn't. He had grown dependant on his diary to tell him what he liked and what he didn't like. And yet, there was something so horrifying about being controlled by a small book, hand-written, especially when you were unable to recognize your own handwriting. And so it was that August tossed his diary into a trashcan and walked up the stairs to his girlfriends', best friends' apartment.

Upon entering the apartment, August noticed that there seemed to be pictures missing. There were spots where pictures had obviously once rested. Dust had settled on the walls all around the pictures, which meant that they had been there until recently, very recently. And then, as quickly as that thought had entered August's mind, it took an equally expedient exit. August was hungry.

"I am absolutely starving."

"Well, then we need to make some food."

The two lovebirds made their way into the kitchen where they would fix themselves a snack. Monica piled sliced turkey on top of two slices of thick sliced, whole wheat bread, which had been previously slathered with mayonnaise, real mayonnaise, not salad dressing, and garnished with two crisp leaves of lettuce. She handed the sandwich to her boyfriend and then repeated the entire process all over again for herself. The two sat on high back bar stools and ate their lunch, which they washed down with two tall glasses of milk.

After they had devoured the sandwiches, finished their milk, and topped it off with a couple of girl-guide cookies, the two decided to lie down and have a little nap.

Of course, if you've been following along, you will know that this will result in the reset switch being pushed inside August's head. You will also know that August is likely to wake up slightly confused. The only thing that kept August placated this time when he awoke was that there was a very attractive, vibrant young woman wrapped around his body. And as such, August was actually perfectly alright with not knowing what was going on around him, so long as he was pressed up against this radiant beauty. He awoke quite some time before she did, and spent that time in silent contemplation. He was not actually contemplating very much because there was not really much to contemplate. He didn't know who he was. But when you wake up next to a woman, you generally don't ask any questions. You just go with it. So he just went with it.

When Monica awoke, she felt as though someone was looking at her. She felt as though someone was watching her. It might have been the reason that she awoke. It is difficult to sleep while someone is watching you, and Monica awoke with this feeling. Once she awoke, she discovered that the individual watching her was August, and then she felt okay.

"Have you been watching me for a long time?"

"Not so long. Just since I woke up."

"And how long ago was that?"

"I don't know. Probably an hour or more."

"Why didn't you get up and make me breakfast in bed?"

There were several reasons that August had not arisen to make his lovely girlfriend breakfast in bed. First, he did not know that this was his girlfriend. Secondly, he did not know where he was. It was entirely possible that this was not his house and as such, someone might take offense to the fact that this strange man was up cooking in their kitchen. Finally, August had no idea what breakfast in bed was or that it was a common thing for couples.

"I dunno. I didn't think of it I guess."

"Mmmmm." Monica nuzzled her nose into this neck and closed her eyes. She felt very secure in August's arms. She felt as though nothing could possibly hurt her.

"Just a quick question."

"Of course."

"My name is…"

"Right. You don't remember anything do you?"

"No. I don't."

"Where to start?"

"Well, the name would be nice. And then I figure we can just go from there."

"Alright. Your name is August."

This was a good start. It was a great start. It was a fantastic way to begin everything. But August yearned for more.

"Check. And you are?"

Monica never ceased to be just a little bit hurt when he didn't know who she was. She knew that it didn't mean he didn't love her. Sure, he had never said he loved her, but she thought she loved him and she felt as though the feeling was mutual.

"I'm Monica. I'm your girlfriend."

"I'm sorry. I didn't know."

"Its alright. There's no way you could have known. You're an amnesiac."

August pondered this new piece of information. He was an amnesiac. He thought about all the repercussions of this. He thought about what it meant. He thought about how it would affect his life. He thought about how it would change everything that he knew, which was very little. And then he asked the question that was now most important to him.

"What exactly is amnesia?"

Monica laughed. August frowned. Monica apologized. August smiled a little. Monica kissed her way from his earlobe to his... well... she kissed her way down. August smiled a lot and forgot that he was an amnesiac. After... that, August once more asked what an amnesiac was.

"An amnesiac is someone who has in some way lost their memory. You lose your memory every time that you sleep."

"Wait a minute. Are you saying that every time I fall asleep I'm going to wake up and have no idea who I am?"

"Yes. That would be exactly true."

"Well, shit."

August began to consider all the problems with this particular situation. And it was at this time that August came up with a genius idea.

"What if I made a diary of all the important things in my life" What if I listed what I liked, what I didn't like, who I knew and details about them? Then, when I woke up, I could just read my book and it would tell me everything I needed to know."

"There's one in the garbage downstairs that you could use."

"What?"

"You had a diary that told you all of these things. You threw it in the garbage this morning."

"Why would I throw it in the garbage?"

"Well, I'm not one hundred percent sure. But, I think, that you threw it away because you felt as though it was controlling your life."

"Interesting."

Now August thought more about his situation. It did not make him very happy. In fact, it actually made him rather sad. It made him want to cry a little, but he also had to pee a little so he chose the latter and got up to go to the bathroom. After wandering through the other rooms, in his quest for the bathroom, he finally discovered one room that had a toilet in it and he assumed, rightly so, that it was the bathroom. After using the facilities, August became curious about the habitants of the home in which he was now staying. So he rooted through the medicine cabinet. He found prescriptions for two people. The two people were Dilbert Douglas and Ellen Duncan.

"So, your friends are Ellen Duncan and Dilbert Douglas?"

"What?"

Suddenly, Monica was terrified. Had he remembered? Did he know? Was he going to go back to Ellen?

"Well, I happened to see in the medicine cabinet that there were prescriptions for two people named Dilbert Douglas and Ellen Duncan. I just figured since aside from your name and my name, these were the only names I knew, I would throw them out there."

"Ahh... gotcha. Yes, those are my friends."

"Where are they now?"

"I don't know. Ellen travels a fair amount. Sometimes I don't see her for weeks at a time. And I don't know about Dilbert."

August thought that this all seemed very weird. It seemed like a very confusing situation. Then he also thought that almost any situation would be a weird situation for him because he had no idea what was going on.

"So, what do you want to do today?"

"I don't know. It's your first day on earth. What would you like to do?"

August didn't know what he wanted to do. He didn't know what his choices were and this was always a difficult situation. When someone asks what you want to do, it is so important that they provide you with options. Like, when you want to go out to dinner, you need to say, 'here are the places I would like to go to dinner. What do you think about those choices?' When you just say, 'would you like to go out for dinner? Where?', it annoys the shit out of people. Well, it annoys the shit out of me.

"I don't know. Give me some options."

The two decided to travel throughout the city, exploring the neighborhood and providing August with an experience of the city. They walked the streets that August had walked a million times, unbeknownst to him, and discovered things that he had once known and now knew again. For example, August liked street vendor hot dogs, but only if they were steamed, he didn't like the barbequed versions. He got two hot dogs so that he could proceed with some variations on condiment choice. On his first hot dog he sort of built a flavor grid. He used ketchup only for a quarter of the dog, then used ketchup and relish for the next quarter. For the third quarter he added mustard to the mix and finally on the fourth quarter he went with all of the aforementioned condiments and added a small heap of onions and a few bacon bits. He ate the hot dog delicately, one quarter at a time, savoring each flavor and determining what he liked. Although no single quarter combined ketchup, relish, onions and a few bacon bits, he decided that this was his favorite and proceeded to eat his second hot dog using this combination of flavors. He enjoyed it thoroughly.

August also seemed to have a distinct fear of dogs. And not your typical, German Sheppard, Rottweiler, pit-bull fears, but rather, he was afraid of all dogs, including shitsu's and poodles. He was also extremely afraid of Weiner dogs, which was an interesting thing to be afraid of while you are eating a hot dog. Monica, on the other hand, loved dogs. This meant that every time that a dog was anywhere near them, Monica would call the dog over while August cowered in fear.

"Why the fear of dogs?"

"I don't know. Why do you like dogs?"

"I find them to be very beautiful, very soothing."

"Well, I find them to be very terrifying and very scary, so I guess we will just have to agree to disagree."

With that the two made their way through the stores and shops of the neighborhood that surrounded Ellen Duncan and Dilbert Douglas's lovely little apartment. They entered a shop that sold shoes and looked at approximately seventy-four pairs of women's shoes. You might think that this is an exaggeration. It is not. They looked at almost every single pair of shoes that the store had, all for Monica to decide that they simply didn't have the shoe that she was looking for. August decided that she was possibly crazy and clearly unstable, at least when it came to shoes and shopping.

After their experience in the shoe store, they made their way to a record store where they bought two Bob Marley albums, despite the fact that none of the four of them owned a record player, and a Hootie and The Blowfish compact disc, they did in fact have a cd player. They then made their way into a sporting good store. Monica felt as though August needed a hat. They cruised through the one hundred and thirty eight Boston Red Sox hats and decided that they were too tacky and predictable. Then they found forty-seven Boston Celtics hats and another twenty-six Boston Bruins hats. They decided that August was not a Boston sports fan. He looked through a myriad of hats and they finally decided upon a Golden State Warriors chapeau. It looked quite charming on him and both he and Monica thought that it looked fantastic.

They left the store and wandered to a park. They sat on a small green bench and watched pigeons eat and kids play. There were a large number of dogs, once more thrilling for Monica and terrifying for August, in the park and they sat there for quite some time watching all of this take place. After about thirty minutes of dog, pigeon and child watching, the two decided that they should head back to the apartment. All told they had been away for about three hours and August was beginning to get hungry. While he did not put the information provided and the feelings he had all together, Monica did and realized that unless she wanted to deal with another diabetic attack, she should get him some food. But she had to figure out a way to test his insulin. Then it struck her. Like a mac truck. I know. Ridiculous.

Dilbert was a diabetic. He had a blood sugar tester. He had insulin. She had heard Ellen describe how she used to have to inject Dilbert and felt that based upon that she should be able to do it herself.

"We should test your insulin levels."

"How do we do that?"

"Well, Dilbert, the guy who lives here, is also a diabetic and he has equipment here that we can use to test your blood sugar levels and figure out how we need to adjust it."

"That's really weird that I'm a diabetic and he's a diabetic. I can't wait to meet him."

"Yeah. That'll be a treat." Insert nervous laughter here.

They entered the apartment and Monica made her way to the bathroom to procure the insulin testing equipment. August meanwhile waited in the living room. He glanced through magazines, though some coffee table books and finally picked up a photo album. He opened it and found himself staring at a picture of himself sitting on a park bench, a very familiar park bench, with Monica. He was still looking at that picture when Monica came into the room.

"Let me explain."

"Okay. Go."

Monica had no idea what to say. She didn't know how to explain. She didn't know where to begin.

August stared at her, waiting. She stood there, staring back at him, waiting. The two of them stood, looking at each other, waiting. Finally, Monica struck August in the back of the head with a candlestick that had been sitting on the table behind him.

When August awoke, he had a vicious headache, but his hair was being tenderly stroked by a beautiful young woman and this made his headache far less painful.

"What happened?"

"You fell and bumped your head. How do you feel?"

"I feel like I fell and bumped my head."

"Well, that sounds about right."

August looked around the room, making an attempt to get his bearings. He found the apartment to be nicely decorated, comfortable, indicating that either he or this lovely stroker of hair was in fact fairly well off. Of course, he didn't know what to call her, so he started with sweetie and worked his way through a variety of pleasant nomenclatures.

"August, are you feeling alright?"

August looked around the room briefly and upon determining that there was in fact no one else in the room who might possibly be called by that name, he responded.

"I feel okay. The only real problem I have right now is that I'm not so sure I can remember anything."

"What do you mean? You can't remember what?"

"Well, I definitely don't know what your name is. I also am not sure what my name is, nor do I remember anything else about me."

"Oh baby, that's awful. You don't remember anything? You don't remember who I am?"

"Not so much."

"Well, let's start from the beginning and work our way up from there."

Monica started at the beginning. She started with who she was, Monica. She then went on to who he was, August. She explained that this was their apartment where they lived together. She was a waitress and August was a trust-fund child whose parents mostly paid for the lavish lifestyle to which they had become accustomed. August followed the story while continuing to survey his surroundings. It seemed a very plausible story. On the walls and tables sat pictures of the two of them, standing or sitting and smiling happily beside one another. So, the story was likely true.

"So what do you think about all that," she asked him when her story was complete.

"It sounds great. I'm starved."

While this did not seem like the atypical reaction of someone who has just been told what their life is all about, who they are, and who they are with, Monica did not wish to rock the boat and thus decided it was best to just go ahead and make him some breakfast. Monica went into the kitchen and August followed along. He watched her open drawer after drawer, looking for utensils. He watched her open the wrong cabinet on more than one occasion looking for a pan, and upon opening the fridge she seemed to be searching an awful long time for the eggs. It was as if she had no idea where anything was, which would be odd for someone who lived there regularly. Thus, the wheels began to turn inside August's head. Thoughts began to fire inside his amazingly jumbled brain. He began to think, 'what if this woman is a serial killer? What if she is some sort of crazy robot assassin who has been designed to look like my girlfriend but wasn't programmed with information such as where the eggs and frying pan are located?' These thoughts made August feel supremely uncomfortable. They made him feel like picking up the rolling pin located just to his left, striking 'Monica' hard across the back of the head and running screaming from the apartment, but then he realized that he didn't know where he was and it would be a very difficult run, not knowing where you were running to, nor where you were running from and likely ending up exactly where you were running from in the first place. So, instead, he decided to wait it out and see what happens.

"Do you like green peppers in your omelet?"

"I don't know, do I?"

"Good point."

Monica continued to work her way through the kitchen, learning as she went where everything was. She made two delicious omelets, one with green peppers and one without, and the two young lovers made their way into the formal dining area to eat.

August ate hungrily, gulping down huge portions at a time of omelet with green pepper, (turns out he did like it), while Monica ate slowly, measuring out each delicious bite with certainty and finality. There was little talk while the two ate, both not realizing until they began just how hungry they really were, and after the meal, Monica collected the plates and made her way to the sink to do the dishes. It took her a great while to find the washcloths, which Ellen left in a very peculiar spot, and begin washing, but August did not notice this time, too busy acquainting himself with his new home.

August got up and walked into the living room. He learned from a collection of photos, that he had traveled to Disney World and was present at at least one game of the World Series when the Red Sox broke the curse. He discovered that his favorite color was likely blue, at least that's what the pictures seemed to indicate given his choice of clothing. He discovered that on occasion he grew a moustache and at least once a beard. He also discovered that Monica was shockingly beautiful. Sure, he had noticed her beauty in person, but some of the pictures, especially the ones where she was wearing a swimsuit, showed how absolutely stunning she really was. He suddenly felt like a very lucky man, whomever that man might be.

The phone rang. Time stopped. Well, obviously time didn't stop. The phone did not possess some sort of magical energy. Instead, time felt like it stopped for Monica. It also felt to her like her heart stopped. She wanted to die. Well, she still wanted to live, but she thought of death as a possible second option. She actually did not know what to do. She could answer the phone. But what would she say. For his part, August became even more confused. Why was no one answering the phone? Obviously he couldn't answer the phone. He didn't know who he was, yet alone who anyone else was. So he assumed that Monica would answer the phone. When she did not, he became concerned and called to her in the kitchen.

"Did you want me to get that?"

"No"

The phone rang several more times.

"Are you sure?"

"Yes"

The phone rang twice more, than ceased. August made his way into the kitchen.

"Is there a particular reason that you didn't answer the phone?"

Monica continued to bustle through the kitchen, drying dishes, putting dishes away, clearly not in the right places, and more or less just pretending that nothing had happened.

"What was that hun?"

"I am trying to figure out what is going on. And I was wondering why you didn't answer the phone."

"Oh, that."

Monica walked from the kitchen to the bathroom, washed her hands and face, dried both, and then made her way into the living room where she plopped herself on the couch, picked up a copy of Sports Illustrated that was lying on the table and began working her way through it.

August followed her from the kitchen, sat beside her and just stared. He stared while she read the Letters to the Editor. He stared while she glanced through the Faces in the Crowd. He stared at her until she finally put the magazine down and asked him what he was staring at.

"I need you to answer me. Why didn't you answer the phone?"

"You've asked me this already haven't you?"

"Yes. And I'm the one with the memory problem, not you."

"Well, that's partially true."

One might think that ducking the question so many times might incriminate Monica in some way, but she was smart. She had used the time to collect herself, to formulate a theory, an excuse, and escape, an alibi. Now believing that alibi to be complete, to be final, to be whole, she sprang it.

"I have severe A.D.D."

"You're kidding."

"No. I wish. I have severe A.D.D. and sometimes I might seem like I am totally following and then out of nowhere, BAM, I have no idea what you are talking about. Like, I vaguely remember you saying something about the phone, but I don't entirely remember, because I obviously must have gotten distracted. So, now you have my absolute attention. Why don't we talk about it now?"

"Alright. Let's talk. Why didn't you answer the phone?"

"I rarely answer the phone. I usually let it go to the answering machine and then just check the messages later."

"Why?"

"Why not?"

"Well, for starters, what if it's an emergency? What if someone absolutely has to get hold of you at that very second? What if it's a matter of life or death?"

"August, I am a waitress. I wait tables for minimum wage plus tips. I'm not a doctor. I'm not a member of the CIA. Nothing is a matter of life and death with me… ever. And if there was some sort of a minor emergency, then it would be up to those individuals to leave a message, which I would promptly check and respond to, if I so desired."

"Well, have you checked this message yet?"

"No. But I will do that right now."

Monica picked up the phone and dialed in to check the messages. Ellen had once given her the password for checking the messages so that she could do so, in case of an emergency. She turned her back to August the moment that she heard the voice on the other end. It was Ellen's mother. If August could only have seen her face. She listened to the message, pressed seven to delete it, and turned to face her lover.

"Who was that?"

"That was my parents. They were just calling to say hello."

It was a lie. It was an absolutely filthy lie.

"Cool."

And with that, the entire ordeal was finished. And August, much like August typically was, was oblivious to the entire affair.

Delores Duncan was now worried. She had gone from mildly concerned, to very concerned, on to sort of worried and had now ended up at forebodingly worried. She told her husband this.

"Craig. I am forebodingly worried. I am beyond concerned."

"Dear, I am sure that everything is fine. She is a young woman. Young women often disappear for some time."

"Are you even listening to yourself? Young women often disappear for some time? Have you been drinking? When pretty young women disappear for anything longer than a few hours, you call the police."

"You're over-reacting."

"Do you even love your daughter?"

This was an argument that had taken place more than once. It had taken place more than twice. It had actually taken place more than thrice. Delores Duncan believed that Craig Duncan did not truly care about their daughter, and Craig Duncan had spent most of his time as a father attempting to diminish the amazingly overbearing mother than Delores had become. It was not true that Craig did not love his daughter. Of course he loved his daughter. He adored his daughter. But, unlike his wife, he actually felt that Ellen should stop breastfeeding by the age of twenty-three or so.

The Douglas family was also having a debate about a young woman, however their debate was not about their daughter but rather the young woman, younger than their daughter even, that Mr. Douglas was currently shtooping.

"I'm just saying that she's less than half your age. She's younger than Dilbert for Christ's sake."

"And your point is? I mean, come on. Some of the men that you've been with were as young as Dilbert."

He had a good point. She had had sex with a large number of bell hops and cabana boys who were likely younger than her son. But she couldn't let her husband win now. She just couldn't.

"That's besides the point you arrogant prick. In plain sight of everyone, here you are gallivanting around with some prostitot."

"That is it! We are done. I am calling the lawyer first thing in the morning and we are getting a divorce."

Elizabeth was shocked. She felt as though she had been hit by a mac truck (enough already). And she was very excited. Nathanial had a great deal of money and the divorce would net her a pretty penny. All this being said, she feigned absolute dismay and stormed into the other room shouting out her intentions to call their son and inform him what a horrible monster that his father was.

The phone rang beside August. He glanced around the room. Monica was taking a shower. The phone rang again. August got up and paced a few times. This was his house. There should be absolutely nothing wrong with him answering the phone in his own house. The phone rang for a third time. August sat back down on the couch beside the phone. Absolutely he could answer the phone in his own home.

"Hello?"

"Hi sweetie. It's mom. What are you doing?"

MOM? It's MOM. How the hell was someone supposed to respond when they learned that a) they had a mother and b) their mother was currently talking to them on the phone?

"Good... good... you?"

"Well, your father is being absolutely unreasonable."

FATHER! My FATHER? It was at this point that August's left temple absolutely exploded. He thought he was having an aneurism. He thought he was having a heart attack. He thought he was dying. He had a father.

"What do you mean, mom?"

"Well, first off, he's having an affair, as per usual."

These were things that Elizabeth tossed around with virtual disinterest. They were things she had told her son a million times, except this time, it was not necessarily her son that she was speaking to, as far as he knew. So it was no surprise that it came as a bit of a surprise to him that his father, who he recently discovered existed, was having an affair on his mother, who he also recently discovered existed. But he didn't want to make anything seem out of the ordinary. So he responded in the same nonchalant way that his mother had started.

"Well, that's no big surprise is it," asked August, not knowing if it was actually a surprise or not but thinking that it seemed to be no surprise?

"Well, no. But this time we're getting divorced."

Fuck. How do you deal with the fact that you have a mother, and a father, a whole family and now out of nowhere, much like that family had appeared, it was now disappearing right before his very eyes, as quickly, as suddenly and as surprisingly as it had all appeared in front of him? So, what to do now?

"Are you sure? I mean, are you sure it's not something that you can work out this time?"

"I don't think so Dilbert. Your father and I have not been getting along for a very long time and I think it's about time that we called it quits. I think it's in everybody's best interest that we end it now."

August thought about everything that his mother had just told him. He thought about the fact that his mother and father were not happy, that his parents were getting a divorce and that he was going to be trapped in the middle. Given the huge influx of information that August's mother bombarded him with, it was not overly surprising that August missed out on one minor, minute and infinitesimal detail. Dilbert. His name was Dilbert. But he still didn't know it.

"Alright baby. I'm gonna let you go now, but I love you and I will talk to you soon ok?"

"Ok mom. Talk to you soon."

August placed the phone down, slowly and deliberately. He placed it back on it's cradle, stood up, walked around the room for a couple of minutes and then made his way back to the couch, where he sat, slowly and deliberately.

It was at about the exact moment that he sat down that the bathroom door opened and his girlfriend walked out of the room, a too-small towel wrapped around her beautiful frame. She was drying her hair with a second towel and as she did so, August just watched, amazed by her beauty.

"Were you talking to somebody?"

"What's that?"

August had learned to play the exact same game that Monica had played with him earlier.

"I thought I heard you talking."

"I was just talking to myself. I do that sometimes."

Monica didn't think about the fact that August would have no idea that he talked to himself sometimes. She just took him at his word, which she clearly should not have done. She quickly glanced over towards the phone, saw that it was in the same place that she had left it, and decided that everything was absolutely fine. So, she wandered into the bedroom, leaving behind her a look that August took to mean that he should follow her, which he did, right after he wrote a quick note on a scrap of paper on the coffee table. It read; "August, you have a mother and a father and they called you at 2:18pm and told you they are getting divorced. Don't tell anyone."

Dr. Wilkes sat in deep contemplation. He sat wondering what he should do. It was his watch. He had let the most interesting, newsworthy unique case that he would ever have walked right out the front door. He knew that it was the front door because he saw it on the security video. When August had first gone missing, Dr. Wilkes had quickly gone to security and had them take a look at the video, which showed him walking out the front door alone. He could not help but think that his medical career had walked out the door with him. There would be an investigation as to why a patient was able to walk out the front door on Dr. Wilkes watch. He sat at his desk and poured himself two fingers of scotch. He drank down those two fingers and poured himself another three. His phone rang. He sipped on his scotch. The phone had been ringing incessantly over the past three days, mostly from reporters wanting to know if he had a statement about the fact that he had lost a fairly high profile patient who had become a bit of a media darling. SO, the phone rang, and Dr. Wilkes drank scotch.

Not far away, just a few floors and a wing really, Dr. DiRossi thought how lucky he was. Days before, Dr. DiRossi had temporarily lost August. But he had found him again. And so it was that he found himself unscathed in this entire ordeal. He thought of how the tide had turned. He found himself instantly moving up the ladder. With Dr. Wilkes failures came Dr. DiRossi's successes. He suddenly believed that he might be moving on up, to the east side, of the hospital, where the nicer offices were. Jake thought to himself that nothing could have really gone better as far as his career was concerned. Part of him thought that it would be best if August were never found. It would work out better for him if August stayed gone. But, then there was the other part of Jake. There was the part of Jake that had gone out to dinner with him, had gone shopping with him, and had more or less been introduced to Andrea by him. There was the part of Jake that thought that August was his friend, that he needed him, and that he couldn't let him stay gone. Against his better judgment, Jake walked out of his office and walked towards the elevators. He hit the button that said up, ironically because it would clearly lead to his downfall. If he really wanted to go up, all he had to do was not push the button. But some people can't figure out how not to push the buttons. So, he pushed the button, waited for the elevator to open, stepped inside and waited. There was that familiar sensation of butterflies in the stomach, although more of them this time, and seemingly angrier. Once the doors opened, he stepped out, turned left and walked the fifty or so paces to Dr. Wilkes' office. He knocked twice and was beckoned in.

About a forty-seven minute walk away, August was also beckoned in. He was beckoned into a bedroom by his girlfriend, a beautiful young woman who knew full well that she was misleading this poor young man. Monica knew that what she was doing was wrong. She knew that she was beckoning him into a lie. She was beckoning him into her lie, the lie that she had been living for the past several weeks. But, she couldn't help herself. He was just too good. And so she beckoned him into her lie, smiling on the outside while she cried a little on the inside. She was sad because she was stealing her best friend's man. But then she got to thinking. Where was Ellen? Where was her best friend? She had asked Monica to find Dilbert for her, and then had just disappeared. She didn't understand where Ellen had gone. Why would Ellen leave after she had just asked Monica to look for Dilbert? What if…? No. It wasn't possible. It was simply not possible that this could be true. Well, probably not anyways. But maybe, just maybe. What if Ellen was having an affair? What if she had a second life that she hid even from Monica and that's where she was now? Maybe she was with her other boyfriend. Maybe she was at her other home. That was it. She didn't deserve Dilbert, or August. She didn't deserve either of them. And she wouldn't have either of them. Monica would make sure of that.

"Elizabeth, you have got to be kidding."

"No Nathanial. I am not kidding. We are going home."

"No we're not. We have another week vacation paid for and we are staying for it."

"You can stay here if you want and continue banging that prepubescent little tart, but I am going to go home and start the paperwork on our divorce."

Nathanial stormed out of the room and down to the bar of the hotel. He ordered a glass of scotch, two fingers, and gulped it down quickly. He then asked for another drink, three fingers this time, and sipped. He sat there and he thought. What the fuck had happened? It seemed like a broad question, but it was a broad issue. What had happened with his marriage? He had really loved her when they had first met. She was beautiful and sweet, polite and interesting. They had met at university. Nathanial was a business major and Elizabeth had been an art major. She was a wonderful artist. He was on a tour of the university's museum when he had first set eyes on her.

She was gorgeous. She was absolutely gorgeous. They became fast friends and it was not long before they were dating and not long after that before they were engaged. They were married in the fall. Much of his family was not around so it was a small wedding. Following the wedding, which took place four months after they had both graduated, he took a job at a local bank. Elizabeth took her own job, part-time, as a tour guide at the university museum. And she stopped painting.

That she stopped painting was the beginning of the end for them. She wasn't happy, and when she wasn't happy, he wasn't happy. You need something that keeps you who you are. If you can't keep yourself, you will lose absolutely everything. And this is where they started losing everything. She stopped painting and he stopped loving her. It was a rather drastic change, but it was a change nonetheless.

And this was the beginning of the end. He worked longer and drank more; she worked less, and drank way more. The two were heavily self-medicated and incredibly distant. He started going on business trips. She started going on pleasure trips. He started meeting people. She started meeting people. And eventually, the two of them realized that they were more interested in the people that they were running towards than the people they were running away from.

He could still remember the first time that he had sex with another woman. It was pleasant. That might seem like a very odd thing to say. I mean, of all the times that I've had sex, almost all of them were more than pleasant. There were a couple that were disastrous. For example, it is absolutely impossible to have sex inside a one-person shower when you are a two-person person. It results in cramping and it results in a mess. So, most of them were pleasant. And the first time that Nathanial had sex with a woman other than his wife, after his marriage, it was pleasant. It was pleasant at best, because it was without love.

On the other hand, Elizabeth remembered the first man she kissed, other than her husband, after her wedding. It had tasted sour. It had not been very pleasant. She tasted like too much wine and he tasted like too much whiskey. And it didn't taste like love. It tasted sour. And love doesn't taste like whiskey, usually.

Nathanial thought about all these things as he sat at the bar, drinking very expensive scotch in his very expensive suit in the bar located in the lobby of this very expensive hotel. And he thought of how much he wanted to go back to making thousands less a month and loving much more every day. He wanted to go back to when they had first had Dilbert. Dilbert had been an absolute blessing. His father loved him desperately. But when things stopped working between him and Elizabeth, he was around less and less and so Dilbert grew up more or less without a father.

And Elizabeth wandered from cruise to cruise, vacation to vacation and as such, Dilbert grew up more or less without a mother. It was amazing that Dilbert survived at all given the fact that he grew up more or less without parents. It allowed him a great deal of independence. It allowed him to make his own choices and, luckily for all parties involved, he had made the right ones. Mr. Douglas was proud of his son. He was very proud. And it was at this moment, after several glasses of scotch, that he felt an intense need to talk to his son, to tell him that he loved him, and ask for his forgiveness for being a very poor excuse for a father.

He took his cell phone out of his jacket pocket and started to dial.

"Fuck."

He had forgotten his own son's phone number. This was embarrassing. He didn't have it saved in his phone, or his memory, and he felt ashamed. There was only one person who would have his son's phone number. And that one person was his wife, the one person he didn't want to have to deal with right now. He was ashamed at what he had become. He was ashamed that he was no longer a good husband, but there was only one way that he could fix that. There was only one way he could fix things. There was only one way he could get his son's number. And there was only one way that he could fix everything. He picked up the glass of scotch sitting in front of him on the bar. There were still two fingers left in the glass and he seriously contemplated finishing it off. Then he thought again. Scotch had probably not helped him at any previous point in his relationship with Elizabeth, and he doubted that this time was any different. So, he sat the glass back down on the bar and began a long, slow, lonely walk back up to his hotel room.

Meanwhile, thousands of miles away on an entirely different continent, the Duncan family was having a very different, yet very similar confrontation. Mrs. Duncan was extremely upset that her husband seemed to care so little for the welfare and well being of their beautiful daughter. On the other hand, a more credible, logical and correct hand, Mr. Duncan believed that his wife was a nut bar and that his beautiful daughter was perfectly capable of living her own life. While these two were not considering divorce in the same way that the Douglas family currently was, Mr. Duncan was considering telling his wife to go outside and play hide and go fuck herself.

Mr. Duncan, as he always did, simply left the situation. He was not a very confrontational individual so, as per usual, he simply left the room and headed to his man room. Now, I know what you're thinking. A man room? What the hell is a man room? Well, as a man, I guess I could tell you about what a man room is. There is no specific reason that you can't know about a man room. You may be a man, or you may be a woman. But in either case, I am assuming that you have a room in your house that is yours. I can only assume that you have a room that you go to when you want some personal time, some time alone. Well, if you then littered that room with trophies, pictures of hockey players, half empty beer mugs and a big screen television, that room has now become a man room. Now, you may be saying to yourself, I have that exact room in my house already. Okay, so you have a man room. But you might also say to yourself, I'm a woman. Well, that's fine. Women can have man rooms too, so long as they like other women in a sexual way. If you are a woman who likes other women, then you may have a man room. If you do seem to have a man room in your home, are a woman, without a man using the man room, and are not sexually attracted to other women, then you are probably just waiting for a man to use that room. I will say that in said case, you are doing a fantastic job of attracting a man, using your man room as a sort of bear trap, or mantrap as it were.

Mr. Duncan's man room consisted of a leather recliner, a large screen television, absolutely no trophies, no posters of hockey players and a Super Nintendo. He only owned one Super Nintendo game, and it was sort of a gag gift. The one game that he owned was Super Mario Kart. One Christmas, he had asked for a trip to an amusement park so that he could go go karting. His wife, thinking that it would be just as good, gave him a game about go karting. It kind of made him want to punch his wife in the face and then hang himself, never having fulfilled his dream of going on a go karting adventure. But, he thought that instead, he would give the game a try, and then kill himself. However, what he did find out was that it was a pretty solid game. So he continued to play the game, and not live out his dream of a go karting adventure. He secretly hated his wife because of it, although he was not too secretive about how shitty he thought this particular gift was.

At the exact same time that all these other families were having familial breakdowns, August was beginning to feel quite at home with his family. His family consisted of himself and a half naked beautiful woman who currently had her leg snaked around his following an epic bout of lovemaking. Although August had forgotten who he was, who is family was and everything else about his life, he had not forgotten how to pleasure a woman, that's for damned sure. Personally, I don't know what he did. It was not part of what I asked about when they were telling me about the story. I can only assume that he secretly knew some sort of secret, magical, ninja-like sexual trick involving mind control, a calisthenics routine and a pair of nun chucks. I have not seen this, but I can imagine it. Boy can I ever imagine it.

Anyways, August got up for a glass of water, needing to rehydrate. He walked into the kitchen, poured himself a tall glass of orange juice and drank it down straight. He poured himself another glass and went for a little walk around the apartment. Monica was unconscious and probably would be for a few more hours. So, he needed to kill some time. He plopped down on the couch, picked up the remote and turned on the television. He watched the first eighteen minutes of the news, followed by the last twelve minutes of the sports. None of it interested him. He had passed out for a few minutes during his epic lovemaking session and now remembered nothing. So, he didn't really know about the news, or the sports, where he was, or anything else really. Then he saw a tiny scrap of paper on the coffee table. He contemplated not picking it up, but picked it up anyways. It read; "August, you have a mother and a father and they called you at 2:18pm and told you they are getting divorced. Don't tell anyone." He was shocked and surprised. He didn't know who August was, but this seemed like a very important message. It was also very secretive. So, he didn't know what to do. Who was this August person? Maybe August was the naked girl from the other room. But what if she wasn't? What if he was August? And what if the person he was not supposed to tell about this note was in fact the naked woman in the other room? He had no idea what to do. First things first, he needed to figure out who the hell he was.

Monica felt as though someone was watching her. You know that feeling you get when you feel like someone is watching you. It feels like... like someone is watching you. I don't really have a better way of explaining it. If you do, please write me and tell me all about it, and then, if you happen to get to me before this book comes out, then I might even put that description here. I am not a poet, and as such, I can't always explain things well, all of the time. But anyways, Monica felt like someone was watching her, so she woke up and looked around, and discovered that someone was watching her and that someone was August.

"Is everything alright August?"

'August! So, that is my name,' thought, August.

"Yeah, everything is fine. I just like to watch... you."

"Well, that's neat. Are you hungry?"

"No, not really. Go back to sleep. I'm sorry for waking you up."

Monica blew him a kiss and laid her head back down on her pillow. August made his way back to the living room and sat down. Imagine discovering all of the following facts in the same day, within the same few minutes;

You have a mother.
You have a father.
They have recently contacted you.
You have a girlfriend.
She looks really good naked.
She is possibly trying to kill you.
Your name is August.

COMPLETE STRANGERS

The Celtics just won the NBA Finals, whoever they are and whatever that is.

It was a tumultuous time for August, and he did not know what to do. He was also extremely conflicted due the whole naked assassin theory. I mean, a theory involving assassins is one thing, but a theory involving a naked assassin is even more interesting. Furthermore, August was fairly sure that he had recently had sex with this naked assassin. Well, he was pretty sure he had had sex with someone recently and since there was a naked woman in the other room, he just assumed that he had had sex with her. If not, someone was likely hiding in this apartment who he had recently had sex with, and he would like to find that person and figure out what was happening.

Monica lay in bed, thinking about her man. She thought about how much she cared for August, how much she loved him and how much she wanted to be with him forever. It allowed her to drift off to sleep and sleep like a beautiful baby. Unfortunately, Monica did not wake up.

August decided that he should go for a walk. August decided that he would like to explore his neighborhood a little bit and get to know the area. But when you don't have any idea who you are or where you are or anything like that, you really need to have a plan. You don't just walk out some front door and start storming around. So, he devised a plan. First, you need to know your starting point. So, he took some paper and a pen with him and when he walked out the front door, he turned around and wrote down the number of the house that he was walking out of. Then he thought to himself, 'this needs to be a little more detailed'. So, he wrote a small note that indicated that he did not have any idea who he was, or anything else about himself. He indicated on the note that this address was his starting point and that if anything happened to him, he needed to be returned to said address. And then he went on his way.

Ellen Duncan woke up and stretched. She felt like she had been asleep forever. She reached across the bed and rubbed the spot where Dilbert should have been, but he was not there. She then remembered that he was missing. She sat up quickly and looked around the room. She had asked Monica to go looking for him and she had not heard from him or from her. She jumped out of bed and threw on a shirt. She pulled on a pair of jeans, some socks and a pair of shoes and took off out the front door. She took a right turn once she walked out the front door, which was unfortunate because when August had walked out the front door about five minutes earlier, a noise which had actually awoken Ellen, he had taken a left and was not that far away. He had walked about a half a block down the road and then was stopped, standing at a storefront window. Had Ellen looked left, had she walked left, she likely would have instantly seen her boyfriend and this entire, horrifically complex and surprisingly coincidental story would have come to an end, and that would take this comedic tragedy and turn it into an actual tragedy, without any concern for comedy.

The storefront that August had stopped in front of was a music store. It was a store that sold musical instruments and something about these interested him. He looked at the guitar in the window and decided that he would like to head into the store and give playing guitar a whirl.

The instant that August picked up the guitar he felt at ease, he felt calm. He felt as though this is where he belonged; with a guitar in his hand. He started strumming, his fingers coming to life on the frets. He didn't feel like he remembered how to play a guitar. He felt as though he just knew how to play a guitar. It was like breathing or walking. He played for a solid half an hour, during which time, many people, both workers in the store and customers, stopped to listen to him play.

The manager of the music store was also very impressed. He was a bit of a guitar player himself, having played with a number of bands through the late eighties and early nineties, and this guy was a very good guitar player. He had a wonderful sound, good fingers and his strumming was virtually perfect. The guitar sounded as though it was supposed to be played by him. It sounded as though he and the guitar were friends and they were getting to know each other again, having a casual conversation about what they had been up to since the last time that they met. It was a wonderful sound. And it gave the manager an idea.

After August had played for quite some time, he set the guitar back on its stand, took a deep breath, stood up, and began to walk towards the front door. He was stopped about halfway to the front door by the store manager, a man named Jack Dunn. Jack Dunn was not his real name.

His real name was Bernard Dunsworth. But when you want to be a rock and roll star, your name is not Bernard Dunsworth; it is Jack Dunn. He had legally changed his name when he had decided that rock and roll was the life for him.

"Excuse me, do you have a second," asked Jack?

"I don't see why not."

The two men walked back through the store and took a seat at a small table just tucked away in the back corner. They sat and Jack introduced himself. He gave August a bit of a background story involving the brief two minutes when he was an absolute rock star and the other twenty years when he was trying desperately to remember what it was like to be a rock star for those two minutes previous. Then he asked what August's name was, and the conversation took an interesting turn.

"What do you mean you don't know your own name?"

"I mean exactly what I said. I don't know my name."

This was perplexing to Jack. He had often known and played with people who didn't know who they were, for a brief period of time due to the ingestion of some real high quality drugs. But he had never met anyone who just flat out didn't know who they were. It both intrigued and mystified him.

"How long have you not known who you were?"

I would like you to think about this question for a moment and recall all the people who have asked you really stupid questions all your life. For example, I would like you to recall the last time you misplaced something and when you told someone this, they asked you where you last saw it. If you knew the answer to this question, you would not be missing the item you were seeking, because it would be in the last place you looked for it. These are the types of questions that I take issue with. These are the types of questions that make you want to take your hand, ball it up into a fist and then punch that individual in the face. August decided not to punch Jack in the face, mostly because he didn't remember people asking him stupid questions like that. So, he thought of this as a perfectly acceptable question and answered it as such.

"I am not really sure. I woke up today and didn't know who I was, or where I was, or anything else for that matter. So, I went for a walk, and I came here."

"You don't have a wallet or anything that might have some identification in it?"

August thought about this. There was probably a wallet at the place that he had left this morning. It would have been a very good idea to have looked for something like that before leaving the house. But he did have the piece of paper in his pocket with the address of the home that he had left earlier that day. So, he could always go back, although he now realized that while he had taken the note, he had not taken keys or anything of the sort, so unless someone let him in, he would not be able to gain access to that home again.

"No. No I don't."

Jack thought about this. He could not imagine the situation that August found himself in. Everything that Jack knew about himself was what made Jack who he was and as far as he was concerned, to not remember anything about yourself was to not be someone at all. He asked August what he knew about the guitar.

"Well, it's made out of wood and it's got six strings attached to it."

"Obviously that's not what I mean. Where did you learn to play?"

I draw your attention back to the part of the novel where we talked about stupid questions and I talked about wanting to punch people in the face when they asked them. August was now beginning to understand this sort of thing.

"I don't remember."

Shocking.

"I just know that I like to play guitar and I can make it sound good."

"That you can. You know how to make a guitar laugh. I think you could be a great guitar player and I have a proposition for you."

August was intrigued. It was nice to hear that someone thought that you were good at something, and it was nice to hear that someone thought you could be even better. And he was intrigued.

"What did you have in mind?"

Ellen Duncan had wandered most of her neighborhood. She had

stopped at restaurants, at stores, in a park that Dilbert often liked to hang out in, and finally at the restaurant where she waited tables. But no one had seen her boyfriend. Her boss also mentioned that she had not seen her for several days either. It did not seem to be a major concern, but he just wanted to mention it to her.

Ellen then wandered some more. He had to be somewhere. You don't just disappear. No one just disappears. Not even Dilbert. He was an exceptional individual, but even he was not invisible. Someone had to see him. Maybe if she used a picture of him and showed it around the neighborhood, they would recognize him and she could find her lover again. She did have a picture however, as previously discussed, she was going in the wrong direction. That being said, had she showed it to the manager of the music store, he might have just said that he had never seen him before. Because at that moment, Jack was beginning to imagine what this kid might be able to do onstage, and what that might mean for him.

Ellen showed the owner of the coffee shop two blocks down a picture of Dilbert. He said that he had seen him in there before, but not for quite some time. She showed the picture to the staff at the used clothing store that was four blocks down the street and they all knew exactly who Dilbert was, but they hadn't seen him for a very long time either. The last time they had seen him, he had been in here with Ellen.

Ellen was worried. Dilbert had never disappeared for any significant period of time, but with his medical conditions, with the things that could have gone wrong, with the things that so many people didn't know about him, it was dangerous for him to be gone this long. So, Ellen thought that the best course of action was to go through the police or, even better, the hospital. Ellen needed to go to the nearest hospital, file a report and see if any of them had ever heard of a man named Dilbert Douglas, which of course they hadn't. But they had seen her before. The man standing at the desk had seen this woman before. The man standing at the desk was Richard Wilkes.

"Monica?"

Ellen Duncan did not answer when this man called her Monica. But when he walked up and touched her on the shoulder, she turned.

"Monica?"

"No. My name is Ellen."

"Interesting. I'm going to guess, Ellen, that you are looking for a young man."

At this particular revelation, Ellen was, to say the least, surprised.

"I am. I'm looking for my boyfriend."

"August."

"I'm sorry, what?"

"You're boyfriend's name is August. Or at least, it was while he was here with us. But then, I suppose that you are going to tell me his real name now."

Ellen was in shock. She was in disbelief. She didn't know what to say, and she didn't know how to say it. So she started with a name, his name.

"Dilbert. His name is Dilbert Douglas. Is he okay?"

It was at this point that Richard Wilkes began to relate to Ellen Duncan all that he knew about the man that he knew as August Feducialiter and the man that she knew as Dilbert Douglas. He told her how it came to be that August became a patient of his. He related to her the various illnesses that August had, which she of course was well aware of, until it came to amnesia. THAT, she didn't know about.

"What do you mean he didn't remember anything?"

"I mean exactly that Ellen. He didn't remember anything. He was a patient of mine for several days, and during that time he made no progress whatsoever and he showed no signs of possibly remembering anything. Until you showed up."

Quoi? This would have been what Ellen would have said if she were French, or knew anything of the language. As it were, Ellen did not speak French, so she said, "what the fuck are you talking about?" It doesn't have quite the same ring. It's missing a certain 'je ne said quoi'. But, it definitely gets the point across.

"You were here Ellen. You were a patient of mine as well, at the same time that August, sorry, Dilbert, was. You came in looking for a young man, but you didn't say that your name was Ellen. You said that your name was Monica."

Ellen felt as though she were hit by a.... never mind. She was surprised. Monica was her best friends name. Sure, they looked similar, but not that similar. Why was this man so confused about who she was?

"I'm sorry sir. But I have never been in this hospital; certainly not with Dilbert; certainly not recently; and I certainly did not call myself Monica. Monica is my best friend. She went off in search of Dilbert for me, but neither he nor she ever came back. I don't know why you're saying all these things to me. But they aren't true."

"They are true, Ellen. And I can prove it to you. I can absolutely prove that you and Dilbert were here at the same time, if you'll just come with me."

She didn't want to go with the doctor. She was terrified. She was appalled at the mere thought that this man might be telling her the truth. She was terrified that this man might not be crazy and she was petrified that this might not all just be a bad dream. Surely this was a dream. It was not possible that she didn't remember any of this.

The two walked together through the halls of the hospital, people nodding and smiling at both of them as they walked. It became clearer and clearer to her that she had been here before. She didn't remember who any of these people were, but they clearly remembered who she was. There is a feeling that you get when you know that someone knows you. It is embarrassing and shameful when you forget who someone is, especially when that someone knows who you are. So, as the two walked down towards the security office, the location that Dr. Wilkes was leading her towards, she began to realize that this man was not crazy.

August, however, was not beginning to realize anything short of the fact that he was a musical genius. He was playing with Jack all afternoon as the two discussed an upcoming gig that he was going to play with Jack. He took the small note out of his pocket and looked at the address.

"I should probably go back home and make sure that everyone is ok with this. There was a girl in bed that I left when I came here. I should make sure that she knows what is going on."

Now obviously this particular development was not something that was pleasing to Jack. He had found in August his meal ticket. Of course, he didn't know him as August. But he believed that it would be necessary for him to have a name. So, he decided that he would, at least temporarily, provide August with a name.

"Of course we will take you home and make sure that your family or whoever this mystery woman is knows where you are. But first, at least temporarily, I need you to have a name."

It was an interesting way to phrase the statement. He did not ask if he would like a name, and he did not tell him he would like to give him a name or even that they should select for him a name. He simply said, 'I need you to have a name.' And so it came to be that Jack and August began the important task of coming up with a name for him.

They started with colors. For example, Red. Red was a perfectly acceptable name. Red was a good name for a football coach, or a carpenter. But Red was not necessarily a great name for a guitarist. And since there were no other colors that struck either August's or Jack's fancy, they decided that perhaps it would be best not to settle on a color. Then the two thought about cars. A guitarist had to have an interesting name and as such, a car can sometimes be a good name for a guitarist. So they thought about Cadillac. August actually sort of liked the name Cadillac. It had a certain 'je ne sais quoi'. But a Cadillac was a big boat of a car, expensive and obtuse. And August was not an expensive or obtuse guitar player. His music sounded fast and cheap, and as such, he would be unable to use the name Cadillac. They thought about Vespa, and about Porsche and even once Puegot, but they decided against cars altogether, because most cars did not sound beautiful and August sounded beautiful when he played. Finally, at a loss for words, Jack had an idea. Since imitation was the sincerest form of flattery, they should name him after a great guitarist. So, they thought about the greats and immediately eliminated a few. For starters, you cannot in good conscience call yourself Elvis or Jimi. It's far too conceited. You might as well call yourself Jesus, or better yet, God. So these, along with a few of the other classics, were instantly eliminated from the equation. But there were still a great number to choose from. They needed both a first and last name, and they needed those two names to work well together. Eric Berry? No. Ry Vaughan? Doubtful. Kurt Garcia? Maybe. But no. And finally, they found it. They found the name because as was written by Sir Arthur Conan Doyle of the great detective Sherlock Holmes; 'once you eliminate the impossible, whatever remains, no matter how improbable, must be the truth.' The truth of August's name was out there; they simply had to find it. And finally they did. Joe Diddley.

The last name is fairly obvious. Bo Diddley was a great guitarist, and there is no other famous guitarist with the last name Diddley, at least none that I know of. But the first name is quite a mystery. According to Rolling Stones Top One Hundred Guitarists of All Time, there is only one Joe. But there is definitely more than one great guitarist named Joe. I mean, to suggest otherwise is ridiculous. I can name two, right here and right now, that belong in the top fifteen or twenty, but I won't. I could name another four or five if I were forced to, although I can't imagine a scenario where I might be forced at gunpoint to come up with some guitar players named Joe, but I digress.

I will not, at this time, tell you which Joe August was named after, because it will ruin a very important part of the book which will come later. During the climactic finish to this story, August will perform a song that was originally performed by the Joe of which we more or less speak. So, if I tell you now that it was… well, you get the idea. And so it was that Joe Diddley came to be. Joe Diddley was going to be Jack's meal ticket, assuming he was not already someone else's meal ticket. And the two, Jack and Joe, set out to return to Joe's home and find the mystery woman in the bed.

But the woman in the bed could not possibly be in the bed anymore, because she was currently walking down the hallway of a hospital, about to discover that she was actually a raving lunatic who was partially to blame for the escape of her boyfriend from at least semi-competent medical care.

"So, where exactly are we going?"

"Well, you seem to believe that you were not here. I am going to show you that you were here and let you know under what circumstances it came to be that that you, and Dilbert, were no longer patients here."

The two entered the security office and Dr. Wilkes had the security guard bring up the video of the last day that Dilbert Douglas was a patient of the hospital. They watched the video that showed Dilbert walking towards the exit of the building, and then showed him exit the building. They then switched to the camera fixed on the outside of the building. At this point Ellen watched the screen in horror as it showed her walk up towards Dilbert and speak to him. Then it showed the two of them walk away. The security officer stopped the tapes at this point.

"So, why was I here in the hospital?"

"Well, that's a whole other story."

"Yes, I assume. But a story I would nonetheless like to hear."

Richard did not believe that Ellen would actually want to hear this particular story. But, she was a convincing young woman and as such he felt it his duty to let her know the story of her stay in the hospital.

It is an extremely difficult story to tell and the actual telling of it that took place between Dr. Wilkes and Ellen was a difficult telling as well. It involves some confusion, some retelling and repetition and some choice expletives that I will not repeat here at this time. When the telling of the story was complete, Ellen sat, dumbfounded. She sat, confused and perplexed. She sat, angry. As it were, she was, to say the least, surprised about the fact that she was apparently crazy. This was the first time in the history of her life that someone had actually told her that Monica was not a real person. For all of her life, people had assumed that Monica was a real person that they had simply never met. This was the first time that someone had indicated that Monica was not real and that she was crazy. But, you cannot simply tell someone they are crazy and expect them to be okay with this. It is not like telling someone that they have something in their beard, or that their shirt is on backwards, or even that their fly is down. In any of these cases, the reaction is one of mild surprise. Following this mild surprise, the individual will likely resolve the problem by wiping their beard, turning their shirt around right or pulling up their fly. None of these statements say anything about the person, or about their spirit. When Ellen was told that Monica was a figment of her imagination, a fictional character in a book that was not written, she could do nothing with her beard that repaired this issue. She could do nothing to resolve this issue for herself.

The two people, Dr. Wilkes and Ellen, retired to his office where he sat behind his rich mahogany desk and she lay on the horribly uncomfortable leather couch that sat beside it. I don't know why anyone would spend large sums of money on expensive couches that are not comfortable. A sofa should be marvelously comfortable. A sofa should be luxuriously, extravagantly luxurious with a hint of extravagant luxury. When you sit on a couch, you should melt into it with comfort. But I have set on a great number of couches where I did not melt into comfort. I have sat on a great number of couches where I had to adjust my sitting position over and over again because one or both of my ass cheeks had fallen asleep. This is not the optimal couch situation. You should not have to adjust yourself in any way once you have taken a seat on the couch in question. For example, my ass is currently in full-scale hibernation because the couch that I sit on while I tell this very story is horrifically uncomfortable. My back does not feel well, my neck does not feel well and my ass does not feel like it will ever awake again. This was the type of couch that Richard Wilkes had in his office, one that showed how wealthy he was, and also how ridiculous he was and how little he truly cared for the health and well being of his patients or visitors. That seems particularly peculiar given the profession that he practiced but it was absolutely true nonetheless.

And so it was that Richard Wilkes sat in comfort behind his desk and Ellen Duncan sat in discomfort beside it. They talked for what seemed like hours and the conversation was mostly boring, so I will not bother you now with the details, I will merely inform you of the conclusions. It was decided between the two that they would continue as patient and doctor, much in the same way that they had been previously, only with different names. But of course, Ellen had not come to the hospital seeking medical attention, although that would of course be the usual reason for making one's way to a hospital. Ellen Duncan had come to the hospital to find her boyfriend, Dilbert, and finding herself had brought her no closer to discovering his whereabouts.

"So how do we find Dilbert?"

"Well, there are obviously a few places that we need to check. The first place that we need to check will be your house. We can call, and maybe he is already there."

Ellen picked up the phone and dialed the number to her and August's home. The phone rang once. Dilbert actually heard it ringing, but did not answer. The phone rang again, but Dilbert once more did not pick it up. It rang a third and fourth time, all without being picked up by Dilbert, who heard every ring, and then it stopped ringing because it had gone to voicemail. The reason that Dilbert had not picked up the phone was that he could not. There was a door between Dilbert and the ringing phone and while he had taken his address with him when he had left the house, he had not brought anything with him that would have allowed him to gain entrance to his home. He had brought neither a key nor a crowbar, and while he and Jack stood outside the door, listening to the phone ring, they came to the realization that they could not gain entrance to the home and the woman in the bed was obviously no longer in bed, or she was in bed and still sleeping so soundly that she was not awoken by the knocks on the door or by the ringing of the telephone. This suited Jack just fine, because it meant that August, well Dilbert, well Joe, was his meal ticket and no one else's.

"You know Joe, I hate to rush you, but we really do need to get back to my place and pick up the gear so that we can go play the show."

Is anyone else as confused as me at this point as to the name of the main character? Joe agreed that they should probably be on their way. Then the phone rang again, and Dilbert stood outside the door, listening to the phone ring. He wondered who might be calling this time, much as he had wondered who was calling last time. Last time, it had of course been Ellen calling, but this time it was Ellen's mother. She had become rather concerned about the fact that she had not spoken to her daughter for quite some time and as such was beginning a regiment of calling quite frequently. She had called seven minutes before August and Monica had arrived the day before. She had called six minutes after Ellen had run off looking for Monica and Dilbert. And finally she called as Jack and Joe stood outside the door to the apartment. This time, unlike when Ellen had called, the answering machine picked up. Joe heard a muffled voice come over the old school answering machine that he himself had insisted they use instead of paying a monthly fee for the use of an automated answering service available from your local telephone company. The voice he heard was in fact his own and it said 'Hi, You've reached Dilbert and Ellen. We can't come to the phone right now, but leave a message and we will get back to you'. Following the beep, he heard another voice, one that belonged to Ellen's mom. 'Ellen honey, it's your mother and I am starting to get very worried. I have called you umpteen dozen times now and have not gotten a hold of you once. Your father is very worried about you and so am I. You need to call me as soon as you get this. If we don't here from you by Friday, your father and I are getting on a plane and coming up to Boston.'

The information that could have been gleamed from this message would have been very interesting to Joe or August or Dilbert. Unfortunately, due to the thickness of the door and the distance from the door to the phone, they heard none of this. Instead, they heard Charlie Brown's teacher talking and then a beep and then Charlie Brown's teacher talking once again. And so it was that Jack and Joe made their way to Jack's house to pick up the gear that would be needed for the show.

Jack's place was not actually that far from the music shop nor from Dilbert's apartment and as such they made their way there in a little less than twenty five minutes via a steady pace and a couple of shortcuts that Jack led them through. They walked up the five flights of amazingly steep stairs and arrived at the door to Jack's apartment. Opening it up via a key, something that would have proved incredibly useful at Dilbert's apartment, Jack led Joe into his humble abode. It was a very humble abode indeed. There was not much real furniture to speak of but instead a collection of amps that served as chairs and sofas, two three sided guitar stands that held Jack's personal collection, which he had purchased at absolutely unheard of discounts, and a mattress sitting on the floor with no sheets and a thick, slightly soiled comforter. Off the main room, there was another room that counted as Jack's bedroom. That room had another bed, well, a mattress on the floor, but this mattress actually had sheets, and a barely soiled comforter.

Joe helped Jack quickly gather up the necessary equipment for the two of them to put on their show, and then they left the apartment as quickly as they had entered it, and headed out for the show. It was a six-block walk to the venue, depending upon what you consider a block, and this is where there is often a great degree of confusion. What you consider a block is entirely determined by where you grew up because if you grew up in a major urban center, you would count a block by major streets. For example, I grew up in a tremendously small town where we had no blocks. Then, I moved to a slightly larger town where there were a total of about three blocks. After that, I moved to an even larger city where a block was a street. So, when I first made it to a real city and they told me that I needed to head east for five blocks, I started walking, and after about an hour, I discovered that a block can mean a number of different things to a number of different people. And I suddenly did not like the people who told me I was only five blocks away. So, Jack and Joe walked six big blocks, six real city blocks, to the venue where they met with Sonny, the club manager, who told them that they would be going on in about an hour.

The two musicians sat at the bar of the somewhat shady club and discussed the show that they would play that evening. They picked a few songs that they both knew how to play, and some that Joe didn't know, Jack had him write down the chords on a piece of paper that they scotch taped to the body of the guitar. Speaking of scotch, Joe dropped a couple of fingers of the delectable liquid down his throat and the two made their way to the stage.

The show that these two musicians put on was magnificent. Jack was great, and Joe was beyond great. The crowd was absolutely hypnotized by the music that rang out from the two musical masters. It was epic and stupendous. It was a fantastic display of stringed mastery. Jack made his guitar cry and Joe made his guitar wail. Jack sang verses and choruses and Joe made it all sound good. They played *All Along The Watchtower* and won over the crowd. They played *Paradise City* and everyone screamed. Finally, they played *In The Ghetto* and there was not a dry eye in the house. When they were finished, they spent several hours talking to their new fans, Joe turning away woman after woman while Jack turned away nothing.

Meanwhile, Jake DiRossi was seriously considering asking Andrea out for another date. He missed hanging out with her, which he had not really done since August and Monica had disappeared. He had spent much of his time in quiet contemplation, thinking about the two of them. While he had not spent much time around Monica, he had spent a remarkable amount of time with August and he flat out missed him. Andrea missed August too. He was funny, and witty and thoroughly entertaining.

"So, I was just wondering if maybe you would like to come to dinner with me sometime this weekend," asked Jake.

"Sure. I would love to."

And so it was that Andrea and Jake once more rekindled a relationship that they had began some time before.

It was almost thirty five hundred miles from Boston to Paris, which was where the Douglas family, at least the husband and wife part of it, were currently located. Dilbert's mother and Dilbert's father sat, sober, in the drawing room of their expensive five-star hotel and talked. It had been a long time since the two of them had really talked. And it had been significantly longer time since the two of them had been sober. It had been an unimaginably longer period of time since the two had been sober and been talking.

"I don't necessarily want a divorce." It was a fairly significant bomb that Nathanial dropped on his lovely wife at this particular juncture in the conversation. It was not something that anyone could have possibly expected, most of all Elizabeth, or even myself.

"What do you want?"

"I want us to be happy. Both of us."

"And how do you propose that we do that?"

"For starters, we need to be home. We've spent years away from home, making every effort to stay separate from one another. And we need to stop drinking."

These were two very good points. They were the primary things that were keeping Nathanial and Elizabeth apart and it was with virtual omniscience that Nathanial now recognized these major obstacles to their time together. Love was not lacking with the two of them, but love had been given up long ago for lust and for sex. But they still knew where love could be found, and they didn't want to leave it forever.

Elizabeth started to laugh. Nathanial first thought this was because she disagreed with him. But then he looked at her face and for the first time in many years, he saw the same smile that had made him love her in the first place. And then he followed through on another thing that had not happened in many years; he kissed his wife. He kissed her softly and delicately. It was the first time that he had kissed so softly in years. Every kiss that Nathanial had delivered in the past several years was rough. It was bold and gruff. But this kiss was sweet. It felt warm and it felt nice. And Elizabeth kissed back, something that she had not done in years. For years, every time that someone had kissed Elizabeth, she had simply let it happen. She had not kissed them back. But this time, she kissed her husband back, warmly and softly. And everything felt perfectly right.

"I have to call Dilbert. I told him that we were getting divorced."

"Why did you tell him that?"

"Well, we were."

"Well yes. I know we were going to get a divorce, but did you just go running to Dilbert to try to get him on your side."

"I have a third rule. No arguing or blaming each other for anything. Instead, we're in it together. I won't try to get Dilbert on my side, because we're on the same side. You and I are together, the same way we were when we started."

"Deal. And now you should probably go call Dilbert."

And so Elizabeth Douglas did just that. She called her loving son and left a message on the retro answering machine. "Hey sweetie. It's mom. I just didn't want you to be worrying about your father and I. We've talked it over and we are absolutely not getting a divorce. We had to work a few things out, but we've decided to end our vacation early and head back home. We're going to fly out tomorrow and we should be back in Boston by suppertime. Ok honey. Have a good day." Dilbert of course did not hear this message from his loving mother, because he was off being a rock star.

Some might tell you that being a rock star is not hard work. Those people are both not rock stars and not being truthful. Well, it's not that they're actually lying, it's just that they've never been a rock star and as such they don't know that signing autographs, getting hit on and playing guitar for twenty minutes or so is actually a lot of work. Imagine now if you had to do that five or six nights a week and instead of twenty minutes or so you did it for two hours or so a night. Being a rock star is extremely hard work. Luckily for August, or Dilbert, or Joe, or unluckily, depending on how you looked at it, he was not a rock star yet. Even still, doing what he did so very well took a lot of out him and after all was said and done, Joe was tired. Jack offered him a place to stay for the evening, since Joe was unable to gain reentry into his own home, which he really, truly didn't even know was his own home. Joe took him up on the offer because really, what the hell else was he going to do?

Joe and Jack returned to Jack's humble abode. I would tell you more about Jack's humble abode but I believe I already have and I seem to remember you not being overly impressed with the original description. So, I will spare you that description except to say that Joe did not remember it being quite so dirty. I know what you're thinking. 'Of course he didn't remember it being so dirty. He's a flipping amnesiac.' Well, in this case, Joe very much remembered being here already, and he very much remembered it being dirty, but he did not remember it being quite this dirty. And yet, after a long show and an even longer after show, Joe was just tired enough that he retired rather quickly to his bed where even the disrepair that surrounded him could not stop him from sleeping.

Ellen and Dr. Richard Wilkes made their way from the hospital back to her apartment. They took side roads, roads that she directed him to take because they were routes that Dilbert had demonstrated a pattern for following previously. There was a certain degree of small talk during this period of time, but it was the sort of perfunctory small talk that meant nothing in the long run. Looking back, Ellen could have repeated only a handful of the things that Dr. Wilkes told her along the way. And Dr. Wilkes could have repeated very few of the things that Ellen told him along the way.

They stopped by several little spots along the way, spots that Dilbert liked to frequent previously. Of course, Dilbert didn't know that he liked to frequent any of these spots and as such, Dilbert was not there. He was not there at any spot along the way, and so they continued on along the way to the apartment. When they arrived, the two headed up the stairs and made their way to the correct door. They opened the door hoping to find Dilbert Douglas sitting on the sofa in the living room watching *Desperate Housewives*, the worst show in the history of time. Unfortunately, Dilbert was not sitting on the couch watching *Desperate Housewives*, the worst show in the history of time. He was not there at all.

I know some of you are now thinking, *Desperate Housewives* is not the worst show in the history of time. I understand that you believe it to be well filmed, well acted and contain a great cast of characters and a certain amount of eye candy, both male and female. I understand that you believe it to be the Emmy award-winning classic that it appears to be, but it is not. It is absolute shite. It is a miserable excuse for teledrama and the only thing worse than *Sex In The City* when it comes to demonstrating the evil that women have the capacity for.

So, after not finding Dilbert at home, the two did some exploring. They found two sets of dishes, which suggested to them that Dilbert had been there. Even more troublesome, it suggested that someone had been there with him, most likely Ellen herself.

"How in the hell could I have sat here eating lunch with him and not figured all of this out. I just can't believe that I've been with him the entire time." And with this statement, Ellen sat down on her couch and began to cry. She began to cry because she didn't know who she was. She didn't know who she was, she didn't know who her boyfriend was, and she only knew one person and that one person was the man in this room with her right now who had previously insinuated that she was crazy. It was enough to make a grown woman cry which is exactly what she proceeded to do.

"It's alright Ellen. Don't cry. We're going to find Dilbert and he is going to be fine, and everyone is going to be fine. We're all going to be absolutely fine. So, don't cry."

Telling someone not to cry is a lot like telling someone not to look down. It's a lot like telling someone not to look while you change, especially if you are a woman and the person you are telling not to look is a man. That someone will invariably steal a glance over while you are changing, look down when you tell them not to and they will absolutely continue to cry after you have told them to stop crying is a law of physics. It's not even a theory. It is an absolute law.

In this case, the law definitely held true. Ellen sat there, continuing to cry. Dr. Wilkes tried very hard to figure out something to do to stop this from happening. He was a doctor of course and as such he was constantly looking for a way to heal people. He was constantly looking for some way to make people stop hurting, stop crying, stop doing whatever it was they were doing. If a patient came in and had a cough, he was supremely committed to making that person stop coughing. If a patient came in and had constant headaches, he was supremely committed to making that person's head stop constantly hurting. This was one of the reasons that he had had such a difficult time dealing with the issues surrounding Dilbert's case. There had been no solution and Dr. Richard Wilkes was not a man who was okay with not having a solution. And this was also the reason that he was having such a difficult time dealing with the fact that Ellen was crying. He couldn't make it stop. And it was killing him to not be able to make it stop.

So, he waited it out. And after a good solid ten minutes of tears and nose wiping, Ellen was able to pull herself together.

"Should we stay here in case he comes back?" asked Ellen, more as a perfunctory duty than a real question.

"I don't know. We could leave him a note."

Now when I heard about this, I laughed. It was a deep hearty laugh that permeated the room. I was sitting in a coffee shop when I first heard about this and I laughed so loudly that a woman sitting at the table beside me spilled her café mocha all over the cream white blouse that she was wearing at the time. She was extremely upset with me and I should have been far more empathetic, but I was still laughing so much that I don't think she truly believed that I was actually empathetic. I wouldn't have believed me if I were her. Well, I would because I know, but you can understand why she might not. Anyways, the reason for my laughter was the idea, the very vague concept, of what that note might say. If you had to write a note to someone that was of the utmost importance and they didn't even know who they were, what would that note say? 'Dear, person of unknown origin. If you are reading this note and do not know who you are, then this note might possible be intended for you. It might not be for you, because you could be another person who is in this apartment, oblivious of their life, but it is more than likely for you. Now, I would like you to call me when you get this and ask for Ellen. I know that you do not know who Ellen is, and you don't know who you are, so leaving a message could actually be pretty amusing and ridiculous. I can't even imagine what that message would say— interesting that this is part of the message that I imagined when considering the message in the first place—but in any case, I would like you to call me and tell me that you do not know who you are but that you would like to. After this has all taken place, I would like you to stay very still until I arrive. Because if you don't, this whole situation will continue ad infinitum and nobody wants that.'

While I was apologizing to the woman with the coffee and cream-colored blouse, this is what was careening through my mind, which I hope forgives the obvious empathy blunders that I made during that time. The woman obviously did not forgive me, but then again, I will likely not ever see her again and if I do I am hoping it is not at a job interview or when being introduced to the parents of a lady I am currently courting. I don't think though that I would ever court anyone who didn't have a good solid sense of humor and if the adage is true that the apple does not fall from the tree, then I can't imagine I will have any problems in this particular regard. So, I feel absolutely safe in this particular mission.

Ellen, on the other hand, unlike myself, who thought that it was a horrible idea, decided that it was a perfectly acceptable idea to leave a note. And then of course the debate was on in terms of what the content of the note should be. Ellen wanted to express, in her note, her undying love for Dilbert, her desire to be with him one again and the details surrounding how much she had missed him during their time apart; well, sort of apart since they had actually been dating sort of. On the other hand, Dr. Wilkes was more interested in the information that could be presented in the note in a quick and easy fashion. He was less interested in having the note filled with statements such as 'I miss you desperately and cannot wait to see you again', and was instead interested in some of the things that might provide them with a solution to the problems they were currently experiencing. Dr. Wilkes wanted a memo: Ellen wanted a love letter. So, together, the two wrote a love memo that had all the necessary information to solve the problems but was filled with passion and emotion.

Also filled with passion and emotion was the conversation that Dilbert's parents were currently engaged in, having arrived at their home following a long flight. They were sharing a bottle of wine; a triumphant drink celebrating their continued marriage. Following the quick drink, the two toddled off to the bedroom and, due to censorship issues that first reared their ugly head when I presented this to my publisher, all I can say is that the people who lived both underneath the Douglas' and to their left complained to the landlord that evening, and on subsequent evenings to follow that the noise was unbearable and that it sounded as though the couple were attempting to violently injure each other. I can assure you that no one was hurt in the making of that particular film. Not that there was an actual film made. I do not wish to suggest that the proud Douglas name is involved in any sort of underground amateur pornography ring. Although I will also say that I am not ruling it out. I don't know these people enough to know either way if they are involved in the industry or not. If I were indicted and asked to testify about this particular issue, I would have to say that I am unable to answer that question one way or the other. I would have to say that I do not know enough to make a decision, one way or another, about the issue of the Douglas underground pornography ring.

Following this bout of epic lovemaking, the two elder Douglas' retired to the sitting room to talk and to replenish liquids.

"Have you talked to Dilbert in the past few days?" asked the family patron.

"Not since the last time that I told you about."

"And he hasn't tried to call us or anything. That's a little weird, don't you think?"

"Well, he's a busy young man. I'm sure everything is fine. But if it makes you feel better, I will give him a call now."

Elizabeth walked across the room to the phone at the same time that Ellen walked across the room to the door. She picked up the phone and dialed as Ellen walked out the front door. As Ellen bolted the lock, she heard the familiar sound of the phone ringing. Panicked, she opened up her purse and dug for the keys as the first round of ringing stopped. She grabbed the keys from her purse and inserted into the lock of the door as the second ring stopped. She turned the key and sprinted across the room to the telephone on the third ring and picked it up just as the fourth was ending.

"Hello?" pleaded Ellen into the phone.

Meanwhile, several blocks away, Jack and Joe were practicing for what they felt would be a raucous show the next day. They were going to be playing at a spot called Blackout. There would probably be a couple hundred people in the club by the time that they went on, so it was going to be a very big show. Because it was going to be such a big show, they wanted to be extremely tight.

"Jack, what's the biggest show you've ever played?"

"One time, quite a while ago now, I had to fill in for the lead guitarist for a pretty popular band when he broke his hand. They didn't want to cancel the show, and I had done some studio work with them, so I played for them then. It was a stadium show and there were twenty thousand people there. That was definitely the biggest show that I have ever played."

"Wow. Twenty thousand is an awful lot of people. How did the show go?"

"It was great." With this simple statement, Jack made somewhat clear that he did not wish to pursue this particular line of questioning and Joe, having recently discovered some of the intricacies of human interaction, obliged.

Several blocks away, Jake DiRossi was picking up his date for the evening. He pulled up to Andrea's home in his very nice car wearing a very nice shirt with very nicely combed hair. Everything about Jake was very nice looking that particular evening, but it did not compare with how very nice Andrea looked. In fact, to say that Andrea looked nice would be to say that the it was a decent walk from Spain to New Zealand, or that Bill Gates had a little bit of money or that Louie Anderson was kind of overweight or that winning the lottery would be neat. She was shockingly good looking on this particular evening. Not to say that Andrea was not typically a very attractive young woman, but very few people dress to impress when they work in a hospital cafetorium. I don't blame them. For example, when I am going to the Laundromat, I do not dress to impress. Typically when I am going grocery shopping, I don't dress to impress. But Andrea, on this particular evening, was absolutely dressed to impress. She was dressed to impress, surprise, intrigue and arouse any would-be suitors, not that least of which was Jake DiRossi.

"So, I am going to guess, based on the fact that your tongue is hanging out of your mouth and you have not stopped giving me elevator eyes since I walked out of the front door, that you like this particular outfit," stated Andrea as she stepped into Jake's car.

"That would be, and excuse me for the horrific cliché, the greatest understatement in the history of time. You look beyond good. You look beyond fantastic. You look absolutely flawless and I almost don't want to take you out tonight. I almost want to take you inside and ravish your entire body."

Andrea blushed but, in order to please her need to be seen and admired by more that just Jake and, more importantly, in order to advance the plot of what has become an increasingly lengthy and complex story, replied that they certainly would be going out when she spent time getting dressed up like this.

So the two started out towards a little club that Jake had heard about called Blackout. Apparently it was an incredibly happening spot where local musicians went to make their mark. Andrea had also heard about the club and had also heard some really good things.

"Hello, is this Ellen?"

"This is."

"Hi Ellen, it's Dilbert's mom. Is Dilbert around?"

What a loaded question. I mean, as far as anyone knew, the correct answer would have to be yes. Dilbert was 'around'. But usually when someone calls through and asks if someone is around, they are not asking out of a desire to know if that person has not gone on a trip to Venezuela, nor or they asking just out of an interest to know the general location of all the people they know. Typically, when someone calls and asks if someone is around, they want to talk to that someone. And this was the exact reason that Elizabeth Douglas was wondering if her son Dilbert was currently around. And thus, Ellen burst into tears and began to tell her boyfriend's mother the story of his disappearance. She left out certain details, including some portions of the story that made her out to be crazy, which should have been left out anyways because they had no real bearing on the story. Then again, if I were a parent, I would very much like to know if my son was dating a nut bar. That being said, it was not necessary to the flow of this particular story. Some of you might be saying, 'hey, moron. No one cares about your insight on the issues of telephone etiquette. We want to know what was said during what was obviously an amazingly important part of this story.' Well, I would love to tell you, but I can't. Firstly, I wasn't there, so what I do know I know from hearsay. Secondly, have you ever listened to a woman, (or a man for that matter. I don't wish to be thought sexist), cry while they are trying to talk? It is not an easy thing to interpret. It kind of sounds like a wallaby wearing a muzzle explaining a joke to a porcupine, and if you tell me that there is nothing at all confusing about that particular conversation, I will drop kick you in the face. Any of you who have younger sisters, or wives, or daughters will all know exactly what I am talking about. Those of you who have had none of these things, I apologize for the ridiculous nature of my simile, but there is not really much I could do to explain. If you would like to know, walk into a high school, pick a random girl and tell her that the boy she likes doesn't like her and instead thinks she's fat. Then, after she has begun crying, and she will, ask her to explain to you what's wrong. Once you have done these things, you will understand the depth and breadth of the conversation that took place on the phone between Ellen and Mrs. Douglas. What I can tell you is that following this conversation, Elizabeth Douglas walked into the other room, told her husband that their son was missing and that they needed to book an immediate flight to Boston.

Ellen spoke briefly to Dr. Wilkes about what their next course of action should be and they decided that after leaving the note, (I still laugh a little bit) they would return to the hospital, which would be their staging point for Operation Where The Fuck Is My Boyfriend. And with that, Ellen and Dr. Wilkes got in a car and drove to the hospital, Mr. and Mrs. Douglas got in a car and drove to the airport, where thy got on a plane and flew to Boston, Jake and Andrea got in Jake's car and drove to Blackout and Dilbert, August, Joe, and Jack got on their shoes and walked to the same spot that Jake and Andrea drove.

When Joe and Jack arrived at Blackout, they found that they would be going on stage sometime after eleven p.m., depending on how the night went. This was fine with them. It meant that they were one of three headlining acts and would get a lot bigger crowd than the bands going on at eight, nine, or even ten. This was fine with them.

When Jake and Andrea arrived at Blackout, around nine p.m., they found that on stage a group comprised of two acoustic guitars, a drummer and a lead vocalist that sounded like a very laid back version of Janis Joplin, if that even makes sense. They found a table close enough to the stage that they could hear the band clearly but not so close that they could clearly make out the band members. They ordered drinks, she a mint martini and he a glass of crown royal on the rocks, and began to sip away at them. He had his hand on her upper thigh and she had hers draped around his neck and shoulder. They sat there and enjoyed the show.

When Elizabeth and Nathanial arrived at the airport, they were told that their flight had been delayed. This did not sit well with either parent. Elizabeth dealt with it the way that Elizabeth typically dealt with things. She hooted and hollered and threatened to strangle someone and told every person that she saw that they were going to be fired if they did not get her ass on a plane within the next couple of minutes, which obviously did not happen. Nathanial on the other hand, dealt with this the way that Nathanial typically dealt with things. He immediately asked to speak with the manager, who came out rather quickly.

"Hello, my name is Nathanial Douglas. I'm the Vice President of Finance for Amnicore, one of the companies that actually provides security for this airport, as well as almost every other airport in the country. I need to be on a plane within the next fifteen minutes and I need that plane to be on its way to Boston. Understood?"

Jerry Billings, the manager on duty for the airline they were flying with, was not exactly prepared to deal with this particular situation on this particular day. Jerry was used to dealing with customers refused flight for being drunk, or customers who were upset because their flight had been cancelled. But, he was not used to dealing with customers who were more or less his boss. And as such, all Jerry could say was, "ok." Then Jerry walked with Nathanial, who was already calm, and Elizabeth, who was quickly becoming calm, back to his office. Once at his computer, he brought up the flights for that day, through his own and through several other companies, and looked for a flight that would work for them. Within just a couple of minutes, Jerry had them booked on the next flight to Boston, which would be leaving in ten minutes. They had even been upgraded to first class at no cost. Little did Jerry Billings know that Nathanial Douglas was not the VP of Finance for Amnicore and had merely recently heard that Amnicore was the company that handled security for the airports and furthermore that some employees of various airlines had recently been dismissed after Amnicore had reviewed the security measures at several of its airports. One of Jerry's good friends had been dismissed after he had failed a secondary security check and Jerry had no intention of having the same thing happen to him.

"Thank you Mr. Billings. My company thanks you for your assistance in this matter. We will not soon forget this."

"Always a pleasure to help, sir."

And with that, the Douglas family made their way to their flight and hopped on. And with that, they were on their way to Boston.

When Ellen and Richard Wilkes arrived at the hospital, they set up a command center for the aforementioned Operation, the name of which I will not repeat at this precise juncture. Richard arranged for a pizza to be delivered to his office and they settled down for the evening to set up a plan of action. They decided that they should start with a call to the local police and news stations. While they had gone through this series of events previously, they had not known exactly who they were looking for. Now they could put up a picture of Dilbert along with his actual name, his address, and a whole list of other details about the missing man. Their hope was that someone would be with Dilbert right now who would then turn him in to the police. And that is very nearly precisely what happened.

Sitting backstage at Blackout, waiting for their turn to go on, Jack and Joe shared a drink. They were seated at a table, Jack facing a television, Joe facing away from it. While they shared the drink, Jack saw a face that he recognized come over the television. In fact, it was almost like seeing double, only on top of each other instead of side by side. Jack saw both on the screen and in front of him the same face. Across the screen a name flashed; Dilbert Douglas. Jack decided that he would be remiss if he didn't try to do something to help.

"Hey Joe. Do you know anybody named Dilbert?"

"Doesn't ring a bell."

"Dilbert Douglas maybe?"

"Nope."

"Hmmm."

So, Jack felt as though he had used due diligence on the issue of Joe's identity and did not in any way feel bad about his slight deviousness.

Jack and Joe got up and headed out to the stage for their portion of the show. It was magnificent. It was breathtaking. The crowd ate it up. Andrea and Jake, along with every other person in the building who was not deaf, which happened to be everyone, were thoroughly enjoying themselves. Jake and Andrea could see the singer, Jack, but were unable to see the other guitar player who was really the person making everyone go crazy. For just a second Jake caught a glimpse of the guitar player. It was enough that he seemed familiar, but not enough to recognize him. He stood up to try to get a better glimpse, but everyone else stood up at the same time, not to try to get a better glimpse, but just to rock out a little bit. He sat back down and went back to his date and his drink.

The plane touched down in Boston about two hours after the show and about an hour after Joe had arrived back home at Jack's place. It also touched down about sixty-five minutes after Jake and Andrea asked one of the bartenders what the name of the band was.

"They're new. As far as I know they go by JJ."

"That's a terrible name for a band."

"I know. But they play pretty well, so I guess it works."

When you think about it, JJ is a terrible name for a band. I mean, I've heard worse, but I've also heard a lot better. For example, when I was in junior high, I formed my very first band and it had some absolutely terrible names. First, we were going to be called Buster Hymen and The Penetrators. I know; terrible. I can't tell you why we thought this was such a great name except to say that myself, and all other members of said band were hormone-filled teenagers and I blame this initial mistake on this and this alone. Our band, eventually realizing that we would sell few albums with this name, decided to change it. We went from Buster Hymen and The Penetrators to our new name, Beatitude. Now, for those of you wondering what would have brought this new name on, I call your attention to the band Nirvana. Now, while we absolutely styled our first work after this band, we couldn't just flat out call ourselves Nirvana. We would be sued. As such, we looked up the word Nirvana (did I mention we were all huge nerds) and found synonyms. One synonym of Nirvana was Beatitude and once we discovered this name, we assumed that we would soon reach the same pinnacle of greatness, mind you without the sudden drop-off, as Nirvana. Needless to say, we did not reach quite the same audience. Following a series of inter-band disputes, stemming mostly from creative song writing differences, the band split up. Those who went with me, those too lazy to actually play music, formed yet another great band, this time with what I felt was a great name: The Jamie McCullum Band. What a fantastic name. I know what some of you are thinking; who is Jamie McCullum? Well, that is a fantastic question. And the answer is... there is no Jamie McCullum. I mean, of course there is someone named Jamie McCullum somewhere. There are few name combinations, especially those including such simple names, which have not been made. Our genius plan was that when we became popular, which we of course assumed we would, people would always ask us who Jamie McCullum was. Our answers ranged from 'no comment' to 'he was a man that we met that taught us what music really was'. These answers were what we planned to give during the multiple red-carpet interviews that we would obviously be involved in going forward. This was not the case, but I feel as though it was likely the best name that we came across.

Now JJ is a fairly awful name. I mean, it doesn't tell you anything about the band or the members. If you know that the names of the band members are Jack and Joe, that might give you a little bit of insight on this issue, but not really. Basically, JJ is a miserable name. I hate it. I absolutely hate it, and you should hate it too. That being said, Jake now knew that the name of the band was JJ and he planned on making a point to see them again.

"Any idea where or when they might be playing again?"

"Not really. I heard they might play here again next week, but that's about all I know."

Jake thanked the bartender, wrapped his arm around his date's waist and proceeded to make his way out of the bar.

"So, how about a nightcap at my place?" asked Jake.

"I don't really want another drink."

Jake seemed a little dejected but was a perfect gentleman.

"Ok, I'll take you home."

"I didn't say I wanted to go home. I just said I didn't want another drink," replied Andrea with a smirk.

Jake smiled, and led her out to his car. And smiled again. And then, about an hour and a half later, following a number of faces that were not smiles, but were sort of happy, and yet looked super angry, Jake once again smiled. Andrea also made a large number of funny faces during the whole ordeal. (I'm not one hundred percent sure that 'ordeal' is the correct term here. If it is, I feel sad for everyone involved.) I was considering drawing some of the pictures of some of the faces that Jake and Andrea made during the whole thing, but there are a number of problems with this plan. First, I was not there, and if someone says I was they are lying. So, any pictures that I drew of those faces would be third party pictures and as such would not be admissible in court. Secondly, I am a particularly poor artist. I am far worse at drawing pictures than I am at writing. And if you are this far in, you are aware of how poor a writer I am and this should frighten you into not wanting to see any pictures that I have drawn. To be honest, you should not even want to see pictures I have looked at and have then thought about, because those are probably about as bad as the pictures that I would have drawn.

Elizabeth and Nathanial made their way to the hospital and met up with Dr. Wilkes and Ellen.

"Mr. and Mrs. Douglas, my name is Dr. Richard Wilkes. I was the attending physician for Dilbert when he was here with us."

"This is where I'm a little confused," commented Nathanial. "What exactly were you treating our son for? And how is it that he went missing during this entire process?"

"Well, that is an incredibly interesting story."

What Dr. Wilkes didn't want to do was say anything that would be seen as 'malpractice-like'. For example, had he said that Dilbert just walked out of the hospital, he would likely have been sued. And the last thing that Dr. Richard Wilkes needed was another lawsuit. Now I know that sounds like there were a lot of malpractice suits out there, just floating around, waiting to pounce on Dr. Wilkes. But, at the same time, I think it's only fair that you know that there actually were a large number of malpractice suits floating around out there, waiting to pounce on Dr. Richard Wilkes. So, Richard had to come up with a story that did not involve him being at fault for Dilbert Douglas disappearing. Now one of the problems that could have reared its ugly head was the fact that Ellen had been made very aware, once she became aware of who she was, of all the things that had taken place during Dilbert's stay at the hospital. So, one would think that there might be an issue with the whole thing. But one would be wrong on that particular subject because Ellen was about as concerned about the Douglas family learning that she was a nut bar as Richard Wilkes was about the Douglas family learning that he was fairly negligent. Thus, the two sides had made an agreement to 'alleviate the truth from the situation' and do so together, thus ensuring they were able to achieve their respective personal goals of staying out of a mental institution and jail.

Now, at this point in our story, I wanted to basically apologize for one thing and complain about another. First, let's discuss my punctuation, which is that thing which I am apologizing for. My punctuation is what the Spanish would call 'el terible'. It is flat out bad. It was bad when I started writing this book, and it is no better now. In fact, due to a fantastic grammarian and puncuationalist, it might even be worse. All thanks to a lovely fop by the name of Lynn Trusse. Ms. Trusse wrote a wonderful book called *Eats, Shoot and Leaves,* which is one of the greatest selling grammar and punctuation books of all time. That being said, I hate her with a fiery passion because before I read the book, I thought I knew an awful lot about grammar. Suddenly I have discovered that I do not. But I have made every attempt, since discovering this fact, to compensate. And much like a minisculely endowed man driving a really nice sports car, I compensated by going a little bit too far in the other direction. I have thrown in extra commas where they have not been needed and left them out of places where they are required. I have used dashes for the first time ever and have experimented—quite terribly I might add—with the colon family, possibly the most misused punctuation mark in literary history.

Now I am not saying that progress is not important, nor am I saying that I do not believe that grammar and punctuation are integral parts of language. I'm just saying that it is stupid to suddenly start using them. It's like watching a movie without subtitles in another language and then BAM: out of nowhere: subtitles. It's important to be consistent, and unfortunately, I am not consistent. But I digress.

The story that Dr. Wilkes and Ellen told the Douglas family was riddled with lies. It was a dirty, filthy lie, but by the time they were really into it, even they would have had a difficult time telling you what was real and what was fiction. They were treating Dilbert for amnesia; that much was true and easy enough to sell but the more difficult situation was the question as to why, if Dilbert's face was all over the news, Ellen had not arrived much quicker at the hospital to collect him. In order to get through this whole ordeal, Ellen and Dr. Wilkes slightly remanufactured the timeline so that it fit more closely with what they said had happened. Ellen just figured Dilbert was off blowing off some steam for a period of time, so she didn't report him as missing until he had been missing for several days and it was at this point that he disappeared, which happened to be the exact same time that Ellen arrived at the hospital looking for him.

"Do you have any video of him leaving the hospital that might give us a clearer picture of which direction he even headed in?" asked Dilbert's father.

This was of course a difficult question to answer. The aforementioned answer to the subject of video evidence is quite clear, but it was in Ellen's best interest that the Douglas family did not get to see that exact video. Since they were in this together, Richard Wilkes took care of this.

"Unfortunately, as a matter of absolute happenstance, we were making some changes to our security system and the cameras that followed that particular exit, the one we assume he took after having studied all the other tapes, was disabled while we made some changes."

Nathanial and Elizabeth exchanged glances that indicated they did not necessarily believe the tripe that was currently being fed them. At the same time, they had no particular reason to believe that anyone would be trying to feed them any sort of tripe about their son. At the same time, Richard and Ellen exchanged glances that suggested that they knew something they were not necessarily sharing everything that they knew. However, since the Douglas family had no real reason to suspect any sort of foul play, they chose to let it go, which was good for Richard and Ellen, since they were most certainly hiding something.

The story went on with details that Dilbert had become a patient after losing his memory. (They left out the part where Ellen was a fellow patient). The Douglas' seemed somewhat confused but Ellen discovered, through a series of lies and misdirection, that she was actually quite good at the entire process of being a dirty, filthy liar. It was not a role that she necessarily relished, but rather a roll that she felt she was particularly well suited to play. Dr. Wilkes was incredulous. He was absolutely astonished that this seemingly innocent, lovely young woman could be such a reckless deconstructor of truth. But, since his life/house/car/job/career/future/bank account all hinged on her ability to be an absolute deconstructor of truth, he was also incredibly pleased by this particular development. It turned out to be a wonderful turn of events.

Elizabeth Douglas sat there, taking it all in, with a certain degree of justified disbelief. The idea that their son, her son, her baby, her little boy, was the victim of all these disturbing medical developments was, to say the absolutely, remarkably, very least, a little disconcerting. She sat there taking it all in, and it was like winding up some sort of wind-up car. When you first start, it's pretty easy. The gears rotate easily enough and you are concerned that such a seemingly simple act will result in a reaction of any significant sort. As you continue turning, it gets a little more difficult to rotate, a little tougher to turn and a little more concerning. You begin to think that the winding of this toy could have a relatively negative effect on the people and things around you. What if, for example, the spring-loaded mechanism were to suddenly and violently snap, shards of metal and plastic shooting out in every possible direction, ripping into eyeballs and through testicles like a hot knife through butter? What if the toy could suddenly take no more, and it suddenly and irreversibly shot out of your hand, shooting across the table, or floor, or desk, or whatever surface you happened to be preparing it for? This gentle euphemism is exactly what happened to Mrs. Elizabeth Douglas as the conversation continued. She started out well enough, but you could see the gears get tighter and tighter and you could hear the gears turn and you could see the look on her face that suggested if you turned that crank one more nanometer, someone would absolutely have to die. Unfortunately, no one quite saw this, and as such, when Elizabeth leaped off the finely upholstered leather sofa, picked up a banker's lamp and shattered it off the far wall, barely missing Richard Wilkes' head, everyone was just a little tiny bit surprised, to put it extremely lightly.

"Why the fuck is everyone sitting in this room, practically eating tea and crumpets, talking about possible breaches in hospital security when my son is out there, somewhere, god knows where, lost? Why is everyone so fucking relaxed? It's not like he does this all the time. It's not like he's a child and he runs away every couple of minutes," Elizabeth blurted out, somewhere between a scream and a holler (or holla if you will).

"If I could say something for a moment." Ellen made an attempt to interject at this juncture, hoping she would be able to calm her down.

"NO. NO you may NOT. You're halfway to blame for this. How did you let a grown man, a grown man for Christ's sake, get lost. I mean, I've misplaced combs, and purses and even wallets, but I have never in my entire life misplaced an entire person."

Ellen thought of interjecting that Mrs. Douglas had in fact lost her husband for quite some time but decided against it at this particular juncture, opting instead to make a relatively benign effort to console Mrs. Douglas with a hug rather than a dissertation on her failings as a wife and possibly as a mother. It was probably the best choice.

"Now, I don't know about everyone else, but I am going to the police station to talk to them."

Ellen and Dr. Wilkes once more exchanged glances, this time also not picked up by the Douglas', and Dr. Wilkes told them that he would be happy to take them to the police station, and that it would probably be good for Ellen to come with them as well.

Both Mr. and Mrs. Douglas agreed to this particular plan of action and the four piled into Richard Wilkes very nice car, the one he might lose if his passengers found out the degree to which he had been fairly negligent, in addition to his misrepresentation of the truth following the incident. Luckily, no one really knew this and they drove in relative silence and with as many pleasantries as could be expected given the situation.

They drove past grocery stores, sporting good stores, pharmacies, homeless people, street performers and the man they were looking for. Joe and Jack were standing in front of a Seven Eleven, having just purchased an exorbitant quantity of beef jerky, a product I can only vaguely acknowledge as food, and a couple of slushies, and were walking out the front door of the store when the car drove by. Joe and Jack saw the car, and neither had any idea who the driver or passengers were. The driver and passengersdid not see Joe and Jack but would have known exactly who Joe was. It was terrible really, the system of coincidences that had led to Joe being a rock star and his parents being worried sick. Someone else who was worried sick was Mrs. Duncan, Ellen's mother. Her messages, because they had seemed less important in the grand scheme of things, had not been returned when Ellen had briefly been at the house looking for Dilbert. She had heard the message from her mother but had believed that it was less important in the grand scheme of things. However, her mother thought that it was incredibly important that she speak with her daughter and when she could not find/speak to/hear from, she got extremely worried and decided that she was flying to Boston.

"Craig, this is the last time that I am going to tell you. We are going to Boston, and that is final. So get your ass in the car, we're going to the airport and we're gonna find out what the hell is going on with our daughter."

"Fine."

Craig Duncan got in the car with his wife and headed to the airport. He was unhappy with the fact that they were going to Boston when he clearly had something else he wanted to do. There was a company that was starting a go-kart business and the grand opening of their indoor racetrack was in seventeen hours. As far as Craig was concerned, his daughter was fine. He believed that if there were something actually wrong with his daughter, he would know, even from a distance. He may have seemed shallow to the untrained eye, to someone outside the situation, but this was not really the case. Craig was absolutely right.

Well, he was actually absolutely wrong. Something terrible was happening to his daughter at this particular juncture, but he didn't know that. He thought everything was fine with his daughter and felt that going to Boston at this time was a horrible waste of time while staying in Burlington, Vermont and testing out their new, state of the art go-karting complex was a great idea. It wasn't actually really state of the art, it was a warehouse with asphalt, which I guess is more state of the art than it was before; a warehouse with asphalt still, but one in which you could not go-karting, which should be the primary use of any warehouse. It is not that Craig loved their daughter any less than Delores loved their daughter. He simply loved go-karting a lot as well. I wouldn't say more, although you could say more, and that would not necessarily be wrong. With Craig, it wasn't a choice thing. It was just the case that he really, really liked go-karting and to be totally fair, go-karting had been there first. But he still got in the car and drove to the airport.

When the plane landed, they immediately called their daughter's house, hoping that she would answer. Well, Delores hoped that they answered. Secretly, Craig hoped that she didn't answer. This may seem like a terrible thing. I know what you're thinking. I know that you are thinking that Craig is a terrible person because he actually hoped that something was going wrong with his daughter. He was not actually hoping that something was going wrong with his daughter, but he did believe that this would be a terrible waste of time if it turned out that she was just chilling out in their apartment. If that were the case, they would have wasted both money in the form of plane tickets, a fee that could have been used to pay for go-karting enjoyment, and time, which could have been spent go karting. In Craig's world, all money and time would be used for go karting. Unfortunately, Delores did not have quite the same exact view on life and on what was important and she sort of wore the pants in the family. Well, they both wore pants, but you understand what I am saying.

Since there was no answer, they made their way to the apartment, simply hoping that the phone was broken and that Ellen would be sitting on the couch watching Regis and Kelly. They arrived, rang the doorbell, knocked on the door, hooted, hollered and whooped. However, there was no response. Well, there was no response from Ellen or from Dilbert. However, there was a response from the upstairs neighbor.

"You won't find them there," shouted down Mrs. Angela Cellini, the woman who lived upstairs.

"What," asked Craig, leaning back to look up to the window above?

"I said you won't find them there. He's missing, and she's out looking for him."

"Who's missing?"

"Dilbert of course. Went missing about a week and a half ago. She went looking for him. Told everyone she would be at the hospital and that if they had any word on it, they could contact her there."

"Thank you."

Craig looked at his wife, saw the tears welling up in her eyes, and suddenly felt a little bad that he had been wanting to stay home for go karting. Clearly his daughter was in some kind of danger and he felt awful about not taking it seriously. He hooked his arm around his wife's shoulder and took her to the car. They sped off for the hospital.

Seconds down the road, the couple pulled over and asked for directions. It seems they had not actually been speeding off for the hospital since they had been speeding off in the totally wrong direction. They didn't have any idea where the hospital was. Now, filled with the knowledge of exactly where the hospital was, the two sped off.

When they arrived at the hospital, they found that their daughter had in fact left with Dilbert's family to go to the police station. They got back in the car and sped off for the police station. (They actually asked for directions before leaving this time so that they sped off in the right direction). However, this time they sped off a little too quickly.

It was like a dream. They hit green light after green light. They never saw a yellow for six city blocks. It was as if everything was going their way. Craig became so accustomed to the greens that he almost stopped looking. This of course was the exact time that he should have seen a yellow. And he definitely should have seen the red. However, he saw neither. What he did see, just a smidge too late, was a car pulling out in front of him. What he did see was the front-end of his car collide with the side door of the other vehicle. And what he thought he saw was his own daughter's face, looking towards him as they impacted. Then he saw nothing.

Jack and Joe walked through the downtown core. Joe had slept briefly and Jack had taken the opportunity to procure from Joe the address he had on his person when they had first met. By doing so, Jack assured himself that he had a partner for life, one half of the musical geniuses that were JJ, which as I mentioned before was the worst band name of all time. Well, it was up there. Walking through the downtown core, they cruised through music stores, clothes shops and a women's lingerie shop. (Jack's idea, not Joe's. Don't ask). A couple of women approached them in each shop, lingerie included, and said they had seen them play the night before. They got some numbers, possible company for later, and continued on their way. Jack wanted them to go home and practice a little, and wanted to bring them to a friend he knew for some studio time. They returned 'home' if you will, had some lunch that they had picked up along the way, something a little more substantial than beef jerky, and picked up their guitars. They played for an hour, then two, then three and by the time they were done, Jack had their next show all planned out in his head. He knew what they were playing and he knew why. Joe didn't know shit. He didn't know anything whatsoever. He didn't know who he was, or who his partner was, he didn't know the songs they would be playing and he didn't know what the fuck was going on. And yet, he was the cornerstone of JJ. He was the musical genius.

The ambulance arrived swiftly. It looked bad, but not too bad. It looked bloody, but not too bloody. No one had died. But people had been hurt. Another ambulance showed up, because it was needed. And the people in the ambulance made their way back to the hospital, the exact place they had just left. The doctor on duty was Jake DiRossi. He had an interesting look on his face when he saw Ellen Duncan wheeled in on a stretcher. He had an even more interesting look, bordering on surprise and shock, when Dr. Wilkes was rolled into the emergency room. It is always difficult to take care of one of your own, but that was precisely what Jake now had to do. He ordered the right tests and made the right calls.

Jack and Joe were getting ready for the show. They were dressing in silky smooth dress shirts, Jacks' purple and Joes' blue, and they were wearing relatively tight jeans, Jacks' purple and Joes' blue. They were basically everything that we all know and hate about pretentious acoustic rock gods. Well, Jack was pretentious. Jack knew that what he was doing was essentially attempting to pass himself off as an acoustic rock god. Joe on the other hand, was innocently pretentious. His character was filled with the pretentiousness of someone who actually has no idea that a flowing silk blue shirt was not in fact cool, especially if you decided not to wear a shirt underneath it, and open up a few buttons. He was blissfully unaware that Jack's long black hair, showering over his shoulders like some sort of Fabio dress-up doll, was not cool and he was imminently oblivious to the fact that his own hair, short and spiky with just a hint of bed-head was actually, unfortunately, and very temporarily, extremely cool. Joe was just cool. Jack was just not. And, if we were to look at the situation in a very logical, legal and specific way, he was also sort of a kidnapper.

Joe and Jack left Jack's house about 7:15pm, which was about the same time that Ellen Duncan and Richard Wilkes were being wheeled into the emergency room. They had suffered a very traumatic experience involving a blow to the head, which was the main concern of the doctors at this point, especially Dr. Jake DiRossi. The Duncan family, as well as the Douglas family, were not currently under his care. While he could see Ellen's body lying on the table in the operating room to his right, he was not responsible for her care, and he needed to focus on the job before him, saving his compadre's life.

Meanwhile, the care of the Duncans and Douglas fell to another team of doctors who were working feverishly to revive all four individuals. A couple, Delores and Nathanial, had briefly regained consciousness however this reprieve in their coma-like state had been brief. Now, they were lying on operating tables, their futures uncertain, their bodies broken from the accident. It seemed as though all four would have no life threatening problems but the quality of life was being put into question by the fact that they were not currently awake, and had no signs that this was a temporary issue.

Ellen was also a major concern. She at this point had regained consciousness but there was still a great deal of swelling on her brain and they were worried about the possible repercussions of this brain trauma. The doctor working on her, and Indian man by the name of Murali Venugapaul, was extremely qualified and was doing everything he could to ensure another successful recovery.

Joe and Jack were warming up. The crowd was getting bigger and bigger and one member of the crowd, sitting there all alone, was Andrea. She was supposed to have a date with Jake to watch JJ, a band they had really enjoyed the first time they had seen them (well, heard them. It has been clearly established that they never actually saw them). But Jake had not called, nor had he answered his phone, and she was beginning to wonder if some ill had befallen her new beau. She was worried because Jake was a really nice guy, wealthy, successful and great in the sack and it was her experience that actually getting all of those things in one person was difficult, if not impossible, unless they were also trying to get a guy in the sack.

She sat, nursing a Long Island Iced Tea while the opening act, Stage Dive, made every attempt to wow and woe every woman in the audience through a combination of skin-tight clothing, wailing, face-melting guitar solos, crotch thrusting and Extreme-esque ballads. They were succeeding in turning on a couple of middle aged woman and one middle aged man, but the general consensus was that they were not exactly that riveting or attractive but rather a little revolting and obnoxious. Luckily, most of the people were there to see JJ and stuck it out. Andrea decided to finish her drink and leave.

Joe sat backstage, trying to remember (still a highly entertaining thought) their set for the evening and Jack was making sure that his crotch was well placed in his jean and that his shirt flowed enough to show that he was very skinny and had a smattering of chest hair, clearly enough to attract any woman.

Jake was beginning to wish that he had been off this evening. For a moment he remembered what he was supposed to be doing that evening and then he pushed the thought out of his head and refocused on the job before him, which was a very difficult job indeed. Richard

Wilkes' problem was specifically with his lungs. In the crash, one of the windows had broken into a shard and punctured one of his lungs. He was fighting for every breath and Jake had to hurry up and get his lungs inflated in order to keep him alive.

Ellen Duncan's head was not a pretty picture. It used to be a very pretty picture, but it was currently a rather sad scene. He face was a little bruised and a little cut and the eye was quite swollen. But what was happening on the outside of Ellen's head was nothing compared with the strife that was happening on the inside of Ellen's head. Her brain was pushing against the walls of her skull and the skull was mercilessly inelastic. The interaction between the two was not something that was going particularly well, especially for the brain. The skull was perfectly okay with standing its ground, but the brain was a little upset about its inability to stretch its legs and roam a little.

Andrea was getting pretty pissed. Jake had stood her up. It was now obvious to her that Jake would not be attending their date and her mind began to wander to the various scenarios that could have caused this. Her mind created pictures of Jake's body strewn across an expressway following a collision with a tractor trailer (ironic), pictures of Jake's body entwined with that of one of the new nurses, Katie perhaps (erotic) and pictures of Jake sitting at home watching Sportscenter, wondering what he should do since he had obviously forgotten their date (idiotic). She figured that option three was not overly likely, and that option one was too terrifying to think of so she settled squarely on option two, which caused her face to turn fire hydrant red and caused her blood to boil, not literally, but in a figurative sense. She stood up from her table, pounded back, rather than sipped, the remaining Long Island Iced Tea and spun on her heel to walk out the door just as the MC introduced JJ. She was not going to stay for this, but turned sideways and glanced back at the stage quickly, just long enough to see a familiar face.

Richard Wilkes opened his eyes and also saw a very familiar face. He was staring directly into the face of his good friend and co-worker Jake DiRossi. He started to speak but felt like someone had sopped up all his spit with a cotton ball and then deposited the cotton ball at the back of his throat. Jake spoke instead.

"You were in a car accident Richard. You're fine now. You had a collapsed lung but I was able to repair the damage and you will make an absolutely full recovery."

"Everyone else," mustered Richard?

"Well, I don't know yet. I have been working solely on you. I don't think, from what I've heard in snippets, that anyone else has actually regained consciousness yet, so I don't know what to tell you."

Richard lay back down (he had tried to raise himself while he was talking to Jake) and closed his eyes. He hurt, quite badly, but he had told enough patients what to expect that he knew that what he felt was relatively normal. His main concerns at this point were for the Duncan and Douglas families. He wanted to know how they were doing and had little concern for himself. He told Jake this, not in the exact words. But more or less, and he asked that he be kept apprised of the condition of the other patients, most notably Ellen Duncan, his former patient.

Andrea stood for a moment in absolute shock. The young man she had grown to really care for, the young man who didn't know who he was, the young man that was missing, was found. She had found August Feducialiter and she shouted out his name.

"August!"

Unfortunately, about a thousand people all shouted something at the same time, most of which were virtually unintelligible. Andrea's shout was very clear, but the masses drowned her out, and August...Dilbert...Joe never heard her. He and Jack walked up to the mics and introduced themselves. Then they proceeded to rock. They were far less full of themselves, despite the fact that they had far more reason to be than did the previous band. Instead, they just stepped onto the stage, raised their rock goblets high into the air and proceeded to impress every single person in the room.

Andrea was shocked. She was amazed. She was surprised. She was intrigued. She was confused. She couldn't imagine that the entire time that they were searching for August, he was rocking out with Captain Chesthair and the Groupies. She tried to make her way closer to the stage, but there were a large number of relatively underage women staring awestruck towards the stage but even in their daze, they were entirely unwilling to make room for anyone to take their place in line. As such, the trip to the stage was an extremely arduous one; one that she would not care to repeat.

The condition of Mr. and Mrs. Duncan did not improve immediately. There were some signs that they were leveling off a little bit, but still no real indication that they would be anything more than carrots for the rest of their lives. That being said, it would appear that they would be live carrots. Mr. and Mrs. Douglas were a little bit better. Much of the damage that the couple sustained was actually to the livers, a reasonably ironic idea when you thought about it, but they seemed to also be gaining some strength and the doctors working on them were rather convinced that they would in fact have a full recovery.

As his parents and the parents of his girlfriend were being soothed by the steady beat of a respirator, the crowd in front of JJ was being soothed by the beat of the two acoustic guitars and the angelic voices that accompanied them. Andrea was slowly but surely making her way up to the front of the stage. She had actually made eye contact with August once or twice but nothing had come of it. She pushed her way past two young girls who were using their breasts as man-magnets and didn't say excuse me, which angered the walking breasts to no end. They pushed back but Andrea's glare told them that this was not an avenue that they should be pursuing. She got directly in front of the stage and stared up at August. She had to say, he was actually pretty cute. She had never really looked at him before in any way other than 'crazy guy from hospital' but she realized now that he was an attractive young man who most women would probably be very happy to spend time with. Suddenly, she was a little like every other groupie in the audience. She had a brief vision of what he would look like naked and then refocused herself on her task at hand; rescuing him.

Ellen's skull was still winning, but at least now her brain had gotten the hint and was retreating. Dr. Venugapaul was excited about this because it meant that Ellen had a much greater chance of living and also of not having brain damage. She was still not conscious, but it was all about baby steps at this point. Venugapaul finally rested. He had been working on her for about five hours thus far and decided that he needed a break, which was probably right if the goal was to not have Ellen die. Everyone needs a break sometime.

The lights went down in the club as JJ inched closer and closer towards the end of their show. They had played some lovely ballads, a desperate long song here and there, interspersed with an occasional rock anthem. They had worked everyone into a frenzy and had them in the palms of their hands. They were toys. They were pawns. They were absolute playthings. And they played. They were amazing. They switched between styles and songs and artists and genres seamlessly and effortlessly, and when it came time for the finale, everyone was ready for it, yet no one wanted it to end. Of course it had to, but not before they rocked the audience with one final crowd pleaser.

You could feel it coming on, like too much humidity on a beautiful day. Sure, it's warm and it's sunny and it looks like it always will be, but then you can feel something underneath it. You can't really tell what that feeling is, but you know it's there. You can't tell if it's good or if it's bad, but you know it's necessary and this is the way everyone felt about JJ's final song. Joe Perry would have been proud when Joe Diddley ripped into the opening rift from *Sweet Emotion*, possibly Joe's (both Joe's really) best work. It started off just a little hollow sounding, like too much treble and not enough bass, but as it went on, you could tell that Joe was doing this on purpose. You could tell that even though Joe didn't know what he was doing, he KNEW what he was doing. Jack came in over top with the rhythm part, but no one really cared at this point. No one really cared what he was doing. Everyone, including Andrea, was entirely focused on Joe as he made the guitar moan and scream and even cry a little. Andrea was drawn into the performance. She knew she was seeing something truly magical; something truly original (I know this might seem strange when you are talking about a cover band, but Joe Perry himself would have agreed that this was not his song anymore). Joe could feel something happen too. He could feel something in him that he hadn't felt in a very long time, or as far as he was concerned ever. He felt as though he belonged, a feeling he had not felt in a long time.

Andrea looked up at him and felt the same way. She felt that he belonged here, more than he belonged in a hospital bed in Boston. He belonged touring across the world making women fall in love. But then she realized that while it was difficult to imagine how, this was a decision that August would have to make. So she needed to get to him. She pushed past throngs of attractive young women and finally got to the bouncer whose job it was to keep people away from the band. She flashed him and was given entrance. She made her way to dressing room A and knocked lightly. She was given permission to enter.

Jake DiRossi, Murali Venugapaul, Richard Wilkes sat at a conference table discussing the future of their patients. Dr. Wilkes felt well enough to at least temporarily resume some of his duties and to assist with these patients. As such, given his quick recovery, it not only made him available for consulting, it made Jake available to help with the other patients.

"Ellen's condition is getting much better from a risk standpoint but not a lot better in terms of quality of life. She is making virtually no progress and she is still out," Murali updated the rest of the staff on Ellen's condition.

"I have started working with the Douglas' and neither of them have been receptive to any treatments thus far. We are starting to run out of any option that doesn't just involve waiting and seeing, which is terrible, but true," Jake was not happy with the progress being made with the Douglas clan.

"The Duncan's are very much in a similar situation. Neither has regained consciousness and it does not look pretty. They have sustained some serious damage in the accident and I'm not sure about any prognosis as of yet," Chris Spencer gave his opinion about his patients but no one really listened to Chris because Chris was what the Spanish would have called Una Douchebag Terible. No one liked Chris and it was evident in meetings and conference rooms alike. It was even more obvious in the operating room, the only difference being that in the operating room, people ignore him instead of arguing with him.

"Excuse me, I'm looking for the other gentleman who played tonight," pleaded Andrea when Jack opened the door.

"Join the fucking club," replied Jack flippantly as he opened the door all the way and called to his band mate. "Oy. Somebody here to see ya Joe."

Joe walked around the corner of the dressing room, drenched in sweat and looking supremely rock star. "Yes."

"You don't remember me do you?"

"I'm sorry, no I don't. But it's not your fault. I seem to have a condition..."

"I know all about your condition August. I know you."

"What do you mean you know him," chimed in Jack?

"I mean exactly what I said. I know him. And more to the point, he knows me... or at least he did know me."

Joe was floored. He was flabbergasted. He felt like had been hit by a MAC truck, (last time probably). He felt confused, aroused, terrified, surprised and excited all rolled into one giant bundle of emotions.

"How do you know me?"

Ellen Duncan opened her eyes and observed her surroundings. She looked around at the room she was in and surmised she was obviously in a hospital. A handsome young doctor stood up from the chair that he was sitting in and walked briskly over to her bed.

"Hey. How are you?"

"Fine," Ellen managed to rasp out.

"Do you remember much of the accident? Everything's fine now but I am just figuring out how you feel and if you remember what happened, et cetera."

"I don't remember anything about the accident."

Andrea stood staring at the budding rock star before her and once more it shot through her head how beautiful a man he was. And she knew that he was sweet and kind and caring. And she said something she never expected to say.

"That's okay Ellen. I didn't expect that you would remember much from the accident, I just wanted to help you get your bearings."

"Doctor, I don't remember anything."

"I know. That's fine. It was a traumatic experience. It might be better if you don't remember anything about it at all."

"I'm not saying I don't remember anything about it at all. I'm saying I don't know who I am, who you are or what the fuck you are talking about."

"I'm your girlfriend August. I can't believe you can't remember that. I guess I can't blame you." Then Andrea looked over at Jack who seemed a little concerned by this sudden development. "The first thing we need to work on is a name. You guys need a new name."

THE END